Teach us to Pray

Biblical Curriculum on Prayer

PRAYERFUL
PUBLISHING

Teacher's Manual
Kingdom Builders

Acknowledgements

To the only true God and His Son, Jesus, who brings us grace, forgiveness and life; Connie Erickson who has stood with me through all of life's adventures; Larry Patrick for his friendship, insight, and creative graphic design; Errol Lester for his magnificent narration; Jim Peterson and Bob Hutchings for their meticulous audio editing and mastering of the MP3 files; Blair Turner for sharing his phenomenal photography; the Prayerful Publishing Board of Directors for their prayers, wisdom and support; Orval Maudlin for his gracious and painstaking editing; and to the host of people who challenged us to keep pressing on to the finish line. Together we can say: "It's not over yet, and the best is yet to come."

About the Author

Dale Roy Erickson understands and lives out the importance of prayer in his individual life and in the corporate life of the church. He is established as a gifted and creative teacher who carefully studies and presents the truth of God's Word. Pastor Dale has had successful involvement in every facet of church ministry in the United States and Canada including children, youth, adult, small group, and counseling. He has served on the national Christian education committee of the Christian & Missionary Alliance in Canada and traveled extensively across the United States as a field service representative specializing in youth and Christian education. He has taught release time for public high school classes for over 5 years. He serves as an example of godly living in his marriage, family, financial and personal life. It is his prayer that this curriculum will bring glory to God and provide insight for the prayer lives of many young people.

Preface

The Teach Us To Pray curriculum is structured upon the various elements of prayer found in the Lord's Prayer. This teacher's manual is part of a multi-platform curriculum designed to help young people grow in their connection with God. The 35-lesson curriculum includes 35 (print or MP3) short stories, Prayer Prompts pages that provide seven thoughts on prayer with the supporting Scripture for each lesson (a total of 245 prompts), an active participation **Student Personal Study Guide**, and this teacher's manual. A **Teacher's Resource** packet has PowerPoint files for some lessons, additional teacher resources, and of course, tests for each unit. The curriculum is designed for the following possible settings: release time courses for public schools, middle school and high school youth groups, home school, Christian schools, and the training of indigenous Christian leaders.

Kingdom Builders
Table of Contents

Lesson Thirteen: Gratitude - In Everything Give Thanks

Lesson Thirteen is the first of five lessons which will focus on kingdom qualities that are important in our prayer lives. Unit Four is called Your Kingdom Come. Each of these five lessons will help us gain perspective on how important certain kingdom qualities are in our approach to God in prayer.   In today's lesson we will review Scriptures that highlight gratitude in our lives with a special focus on Psalms 103:1-14. King David was called a "man after God's own heart," and I believe that one of the special qualities that he had was a thankful heart. You cannot read through the story of David's life, and especially the Psalms that he wrote, without seeing that element shine through. Our goal in today's lesson is to help the students reflect upon the presence or absence of gratitude in their lives, and review some of the many reasons that they should come to God with a grateful heart.

Most people are not naturally pointed in a direction that supports this quality of life. It is much easier to focus our thoughts about life on the things we don't have rather than the things we have. To illustrate this, invite the students to give one-word reflections in response to the headings on two poster boards. One will read THAT TICKS ME OFF; the other will read THAT MAKES ME HAPPY. After each has participated, review the boards and have each learner share why they chose their particular words for each poster. You will find a lot of agreement expressed as the results are shared. When that is done, ask the students to reflect on their two responses and answer this question: "Which poster evoked the strongest response as they wrote down their response?" Or said another way: "Which response brought out the strongest emotion, or which response do they identify with naturally?" The premise is that most of us find it quite easy to identify with negative responses rather than positive ones. The natural tendency is to find it challenging to "give thanks in everything" as given in 1 Thessalonians 5:18. It will be easy to let this activity use up too much time. If time restraints are a concern, have a limited number of learners respond.

In order to set their attention on this attribute of a prayerful person, the second part of the **HOOK ACTIVITY** will highlight the importance of "keeping our focus on the ball." In almost every sport (golf, baseball, tennis, etc.), keeping your eye on the ball is a vital element for success. We will use an interesting YouTube video clip to illustrate this truth. It is located at https://www.youtube.com/watch?v=OAunjLu4LCE. At the close of the clip tell the students that when we come before God in prayer, "gratitude" is as critical as "keeping our eye on the ball" is to most sports.

We can now transition to the **BOOK ACTIVITY**, which will highlight some passages that tell us where we should keep our eyes focused. Philippians 4:6-9 will point us in the right direction. A summary introduction might be: "In order to have the peace of God, we need to start with presenting our requests (i.e. needs) to God, and keeping our mind focused on things that are true, honorable, right, pure, lovely, of good repute, excellence and praise worthy." That is easier said than done as we discovered in our poster board exercise today. We will need God's help to keep our eye on the ball. That is also true when it comes to fostering "gratitude" in our lives. This really comes back to the struggle of walking in the flesh or walking in the Spirit (see Galatians 5:16,17).

For a more detailed list of things that we should focus on, we might look to Psalm 103:1-14. David challenges us to maintain a proper perspective by looking to the benefits brought into our lives from God. In his words: "forget none of his benefits." Give the learners 3.x 5 index cards and have them list the benefits they find in the Psalm 103 passage. If time permits, challenge the learners to read through the list of those benefits and select the one that is most meaningful to them. If the time constraints of your setting allow, have them share why they selected that benefit over the other wonderful blessings.

At this point we have looked at both the direction (Philippians 4) of our attention and reflected on the greatness and goodness of God (Psalm 103). Keeping our eyes focused on the ball in these areas will bring gratitude into our hearts. In case the learners still need motivation in developing gratitude as we come before God, the **LOOK ACTIVITY** might provide some help. Most of the learners who have access to this curriculum will find themselves in a favorable position when compared to the circumstances of most of the people in the world. If they have read their **student personal study guide**, you could simply review the questions associated with the "If The World Were 100 People" portion of the lesson. If not, you might use the teacher resource by that title and help them gain a new perspective. You can find a YouTube video that highlights this truth by doing a search for "If the world were 100 people." The video link used for the Student Personal Study Guide is: **https://www.youtube.com/watch?v=UbffuGZHeR0**. The supporting data can be found at: http://www.100people.org/statistics_100stats.php?section=statistics. The data on this issue is constantly changing. The statistics from the YouTube video are slightly different from those in the supporting data sheet. The data sheet statistics will be given as the first answer in this teacher's manual. The statistics from the YouTube video will be listed in (parentheses). There were items that were skipped over, or not included in the exercise, as they were not as pertinent to this lesson. There are multiple versions of this on YouTube, and we selected the most up-to-date one when this lesson was prepared. The student manual and the teacher's resource exercise are built around this particular version. If you find there is a more up-to-date rendering of these statistics when you teach this lesson, you might want to adjust the categories to fit the new video. Either way, this exercise should highlight how grateful the learners should be for their life circumstance. If they haven't found enough reason to be grateful already, remind them of the incredible price Jesus paid to make salvation available. 2 Corinthians 9:15: "Thanks be to God for His indescribable gift!" NASB

IF THE WORLD WERE 100 PEOPLE EXERCISE

1. In the home where you were raised _____% were female and _____% were male.

If the World were 100 PEOPLE:

___50_(50)___ are Female ___50_(50)___ are Male

How does that influence the way you view your place in the world? _____

_____

_____

2. In the home you live in right now, what percentage of the people are:

_____% Asian

_____% African

_____% European

_____% American

If the World were 100 PEOPLE:

__60_(59)__ would be Asian   ___10_(10)__ would be European

__16_(16)__ would be African   ___14_(14)__ would be American

How does that influence the way you view your place in the world? _____

_____

_____

3. In the home you live in right now, what percentage are?

_____% Christian

_____% Muslim

_____% not religious or not aligned with a particular faith

_____% Hindu

_____% other religions

_____% Buddhist

If the world were 100 PEOPLE:

___31_(31)__ would be Christian

___23_(23)__ would be Muslim

___16_(15)__ would be not religious or not aligned with a particular faith

___15_(15)__ would be Hindu

____8__(9)__ would be other religions

____7__(7)__ would be Buddhist

How does that influence the way you view your place in the world? _____

_____

_____

4. In the home you (or your extended family) live in, what percentage of the people speak?

_____% Chinese

_____% Spanish

_____% English

_____% Hindi

_____% Arabic

_____% Other language

If the world were 100 PEOPLE:

    __12__ (14)__ would speak Chinese
    __6___ (8)__ would speak Spanish
    __5__ (13)__ would speak English
    __4___ (9)__ would speak Hindi
    __3___ (5)__ would speak Arabic
    __70__ (51)__ would speak other languages

How does that influence the way you view your place in the world? _____

_____

_____

5. In the home you (or your extended family) live in, what percentage would be literate?
    _____%

If the world were 100 PEOPLE:

__86_ (86)__ Could read
__14_ (14)__ Could not read

How does that influence the way you view your place in the world? _____

_____

_____

6. What percentage of your immediate or extended family, have a college degree? _____%

If the world were 100 PEOPLE:

__7_ (7)_ would have a college degree

How does that influence the way you view your place in the world? _____

_____

_____

7. What percentage of the people you know do not have access to the internet? _____%

If the world were 100 PEOPLE:

__40_ (42)__ would have an internet connection

How does that influence the way you view your place in the world? _____

_____

_____

8. What percentage of your immediate or extended family, have somewhere to live? _____%

If the world were 100 PEOPLE:

___77_(78)__ would have shelter where they live
___22_(22)__ would not have shelter where they live

How does that influence the way you view your place in the world? _____

_____

_____

9. What percentage of your friends and family don't have enough to eat? ____%

If the world were 100 PEOPLE:

___88_(88)__ would have enough to eat
___12_(12)__ would not have enough to eat

How does that influence the way you view your place in the world? _____

_____

_____

10. What percentage of your friends and family have safe drinking water? ____%

If the world were 100 PEOPLE:

___87_(92)__ would have access to safe drinking water
___13__(8)__ would use unimproved water

How does that influence the way you view your place in the world? _____

_____

_____

You will find the documentation which was compiled by: 2016 - Fritz Erickson, Provost and Vice President for Academic Affairs, Ferris State University (Formerly Dean of Professional and Graduate Studies, University of Wisconsin - Green Bay) and John A. Vonk, University of Northern Colorado, 2006; Returning Peace Corps Volunteers of Madison Wisconsin, Unheard Voices: Celebrating Cultures from the Developing World, 1992; Donella H. Meadows, The Global Citizen, May 31, 1990 at http://www.100people.org/statistics_100stats.php?section=statistics.

The **TOOK ACTIVITY** for this lesson encourages the learners to express their gratitude by writing a "Thank you" note to God. When they are done, it will be a critical element of this lesson to have them read their thank you note as a prayer. Other students can follow what is being read, and silently make that a personal prayer if they feel it might apply. It is vital that time be allowed for this prayer element.

Memory Verse: Psalm 19:14 Let the words of my mouth and the meditation of my heart be acceptable in Your sight, O LORD, my rock and my Redeemer   NASB

SESSION PLANNING SHEET

Session Title: _In Everything Give Thanks _____ Date: _____

Session Focus: _Kingdom Qualities – Gratitude _____

Session Aims: **KNOW** _Identify some critical attitudes that should accompany the requests that we bring to God. _____

FEEL _Express your level of gratitude for the many blessings God has brought into your life. _____

DO _Write a thank you card to God for the ways He has blessed you and review it each day this week.____

Session Plan	Session Activities	Preparation
Time: __10 min___ **APPROACH**	**Methods, Instructions, Questions** **Ticks Me Off Poster board** you could use a big "sad" emoticon **Makes Me Happy Poster board** you could use a big "happy" emoticon **Which of the words you selected on these two poster boards brings out the most passion or emotion for you?** **Keep your eye on the ball exercise** https://www.youtube.com/watch?v=OAunjLu4LCE	**Materials** **Poster board** **Magic Markers** **Access to You Tube internet connection means of projection for larger groups**
Time: ___15 min__ **BIBLE EXPLORATION**	**1 Thessalonians 5:18, Philippians 4:6-9, Psalm 103:1-14** Have students read this Psalm 103 aloud from several different translations. 3 x 5 card exercise from Psalm 103:1-14. Students should write down words that summarize things for which they are thankful. If time permits, have them select the most meaningful one. Why did they select that particular benefit?	**Bibles** **3 x 5 cards** **Pencils or pens**
Time: __15 min__ **LIFE IMPLICATIONS**	HOW WOULD YOUR LIFE BE IMPROVED IF YOU FOCUSED ON THAT ONE BENEFIT AS YOU START EACH MORNING? **If the World were 100 people** https://www.youtube.com/watch?v=UbffuGZHeR0 **If the World were 100 people worksheet** Students should discover how many out of 100 people from each category exist in the world. Encourage students to compare their life circumstances with the people in the rest of the world.	**Access to youtube.com** **Means of projection for larger groups** IF THE WORLD WERE 100 PEOPLE WORKSHEETS, PENS FOR THOSE WITH STUDENT MANUALS THIS EXERCISE IS IN THE MANUAL
Time: __15 min___ **APPLICATION**	**THANK YOU CARD EXERCISE** **Write a thank you card to God for all the blessings He has brought into your life.** While each student reads their thank you cards out loud, the remainder of the class can follow along, and make things they are thankful for into silent prayers of Thanksgiving. Take the thank you card home and review it each morning. Thank God for the blessings that He brings into your life. **Group Prayer:** Take personal prayer requests and have students pray for each other.	**Thank You Cards** **Pens & Pencils**

Session Planning Sheet ©2013 Dale Roy Erickson, adapted from material found in *Creative Bible Teaching* © 1998 by Lawrence O. Richards and Gary J. Bredfeldt, Moody Publishers. Used by permission.

Unit Four – Your Kingdom Come – Lesson 13   Gratitude...Prompts

"Everything" is a pretty long list...It will shape our hearts just reflecting upon it.

1 Thessalonians 5:17,18   Pray without ceasing, in everything give thanks; for this is God's will for you in Christ Jesus.   NKJV

We are made in the image of God. He is unbelievably creative (imaginative). Here's one way to start our time of prayer. Imagine Jesus himself sitting across the room and tell him "Thank you" with all of our heart.

2 Corinthians 9:15   Thanks be to God for his indescribable gift!   NKJV

The phrase: "keep your eye on the ball" is a key fundamental of the game in many sports. In our relationship with God, "gratitude" is keeping our eye on the ball.

Psalm 145:10   All Your works shall praise You, O Lord, And Your saints shall bless You.   NKJV

Dear Lord, please forgive me for grumbling. I have so much to be thankful for, but my heart slides too easily into complaints. Change my heart, O God, and help me to always be grateful.

Psalm 19:14   Let the words of my mouth and the meditation of my heart Be acceptable in Your sight, O LORD, my rock and my Redeemer   NASB

Effectual prayer flows out of the fabric of our daily lives. It has been said: "Actions form habits; habits decide character; and character fixes our destiny."

Daniel 6:10   But when Daniel learned that the law had been signed, he went home and knelt down as usual in his upstairs room, with its windows open toward Jerusalem. He prayed three times a day, just as he had always done, giving thanks to his God.   NLT

Many people ask God to bless their food before they eat it. God has already said that "everything He created" is good for us on one condition...that we receive it from Him with gratitude. It's true of a lot more than just food.

1 Timothy 4:4,5   For everything God created is good, and nothing is to be rejected if it is received with thanksgiving, because it is consecrated by the word of God and prayer.   NIV

Gratitude is a great place to start in our worship. It is an offering in which God delights. The grumpy, discontent spirit gives a poor reflection of his God and Father. The joyful and grateful heart brings honor to Him.

Psalm 50:14,15,23   Offer to God thanksgiving, And pay your vows to the Most High. Call upon Me in the day of trouble; I will deliver you, and you shall glorify Me." Whoever offers praise glorifies Me; And to him who orders his conduct aright I will show the salvation of God."   NKJV

Lesson Fourteen: Humility

Lesson Fourteen is the second of five lessons which will focus on kingdom qualities that are important in our prayer lives. Unit Four is called Your Kingdom Come. Each of these five lessons will help us gain perspective on how important certain kingdom qualities are in our approach to God in prayer. We will look primarily at four Scriptural examples on the issue of humility. First, the example of Jesus in Philippians 2:8-12, which highlights the fact that Jesus left the glories of heaven and humbled himself… not only by becoming human, but in His willingness to serve the needs of mankind by going to the cross. The second example is found in 2 Chronicles 7:14, where the Bible highlights the fact that the first step in national restoration is found in God's people humbling themselves and praying. The third example would involve selected passages from Genesis 37-50, which highlight situations in the lives of Joseph and his family that could have lead to either pride or humility. The fourth example is the poignant example of pride and humility found in the person of Nebuchadnezzar from Daniel chapter 4. The overarching point of this lesson is that humility is a vital character quality for an effective prayer life, and that we have opportunity to choose either pride or humility in situations that arise throughout our lifetime. The person who allows their heart to become proud will find, according to James 4:6, that God stands in opposition to them. It is a personal choice. And according to James 4:10, we can make the choice to humble ourselves. It certainly is a wise choice when we come before God in prayer.

The **HOOK ACTIVITY** illustrates how our hearts are naturally drawn to self-interest. The advent of the cell phone camera brought forward a new phenomenon. It is the ability to take a picture of oneself…either a single photo or in a small group setting. A few decades ago this choice didn't exist. If someone had tried such a thing, it would have likely been ridiculed. This illustrates to some degree how narcissistic our culture has become. This might simply be a symptom of larger issues, but it could certainly illustrate the issues of pride and humility in our world. The activity would be to have those with cell phone cameras take a "selfie." Have them show the "selfie" to a class partner and have that person share what they "see." Ask the person who took the "selfie" how what they see is different than what the person described. Listen carefully, as this will provide you with the opportunity to briefly share that it is "who we are in Christ" that truly defines us. You might note that some took individual photos, while some asked others to be in their "selfie." Ask: If Jesus had a cell phone in His day, what do you think His "selfie" would have looked like? You could highlight several Scriptures that say that Jesus came to serve us, not the other way around (Mark 10:43-45)…that Jesus chose to leave the throne room of heaven to become human and die for our sins (Philippians 2:8-12)…that Jesus said of Himself that He was a "gentle and humble" person (Matthew 11:29). We might all want to be like Jesus in this aspect of our lives, but that might be easier said than done. It is a choice that we have every day, and the great thing is that it's not just up to us. God is willing to come to our aid. If we choose pride, God will be opposed to us. If we choose humility, He will not only be on our side, but promises to reward our choice. You should understand that what you are is God's gift to you. What you make of yourself is your gift to God and others. When we choose to humble ourselves by giving our lives in the service of others, we will find reward for them and ourselves. A good example of this is found in the lives Joseph and his family.

In the **BOOK ACTIVITY** we will take a look at different situations that arose in Joseph's life that presented opportunities for (or revealed the presence of) pride or humility. This is obviously a selective list of his experiences, and were chosen to illustrate life situations that could lead to humility or pride. There are some possible discussion questions listed at the bottom of this page. The student's answers in these settings will likely tell us a lot about them. Clearly there will not be enough time in a normal classroom setting to bring in all of the discussion questions. You will have to make judgments as to how quickly to review the details of the story, and which discussion questions are most pertinent for your setting. Hopefully the students will have used the student manual to review the discussion questions in preparation for the class. If not, use the Pride Humility Possibilities Grab bag file from the teacher's resources to make "grab bag" slips for the learners to review and then discuss in class.

1. Gen. 37:3,4 **Coat of many colors** – Jacob (Israel) loved Joseph more than his other sons and demonstrated this by making him a special coat that set him apart from the others (i.e. more loved). How could that possibly lead to a pride or humility issue in Joseph's life?
2. Gen. 37-5-11 **Joseph's dreams** – Joseph had two dreams that represented his family doing homage to him (i.e. honoring him). How could that possibly lead to a pride or humility issue in Joseph's life? How did his "sharing" about his dream possibly demonstrate either pride or humility? What are the possible responses of people when someone else rises in stature? What does that response say about their predisposition to either pride or humility?
3. Gen. 37:18-21 **Rueben plans to rescue Joseph** - Rueben was the first born of the sons, and as such would normally (in that culture) be the one in the lead when Jacob wasn't present. In your opinion does his plan to rescue Joseph reflect more a "responsibility" motive, a "humility" motive, or a "compassion" motive? What does this plan reflect about Rubin's understanding of accountability (humility) before God and/or Jacob?
4. Gen. 37:23-26 **Judah's profit scheme** – Judah presents a plan where the brothers could profit from their plans for Joseph. Does this plan reflect an arrogance (pride) about accountability before God?
5. Gen. 37:27,28 **Joseph sold into slavery** – Having his brothers sell him as a slave may have presented Joseph with an opportunity to learn humility or left him bitter. Which one do you think he chose?
6. Gen. 37:29-34 **Rueben's cover up** – Rueben lies to his father about what happened and covers it up. What does this reveal about his understanding of accountability (humility/pride) before God and/or Jacob?
7. Gen. 39:1-6 **Joseph's skill recognized** – Do you think that when Joseph was placed in charge of the household, that he became proud or remained humble? What makes you believe that?
8. Gen. 39:7-20 **Joseph falsely accused** Do you think that Joseph's response to being falsely accused of rape revealed a heart filled with pride or humility? What makes you believe that?
9. Gen. 39-21-23 **Joseph in charge of jail** - Do you think that Joseph being placed in charge of the jail presented an opportunity that could lead to pride or humility? What makes you believe that?
10. Gen. 41:14-16, 33-41 **Joseph 2nd Egypt** - Do you think that Joseph being placed in charge of all Egypt (excluding Pharaoh's authority) presented an opportunity that could lead to pride or humility? What makes you believe that?

11. Gen. 42:1-8;17 **Brothers bow down -** Do you think that having his brothers bowing down before Joseph presented him with an opportunity that could lead to pride or humility? Do you think when his brothers bowed down before Joseph that it presented them with an opportunity that could lead to pride or humility? What makes you believe that?

12. Gen. 42:18-24 **Simeon put in jail** – Do you think when the brothers unknowingly admitted their guilt it may have helped in Joseph's response? Why or why not? Do you think when Rueben unknowingly admitted their guilt that it represented humility on their part? Why or why not? Do you think Rueben's admission of guilt had anything to do with his being chosen as the one placed in prison? Do you think Rueben being the eldest brother had anything to do with his being chosen as the one placed in prison?

13. Gen. 43:26-34 **Benjamin honored** - Do you think that Benjamin being honored by being given a portion of food 5 times greater than his brothers represented a test of the brother's jealousy? How is jealousy related to pride and humility?

14. Gen. 44:16-18,32-34 **Judah's recompense** – Do you think that Judah being placed in a position of taking responsibility for Benjamin's penalty was unrelated to his scheme of profiting from Joseph's sale as a slave? How are they similar? How are they different? What does his taking responsibility reveal in the areas of pride, humility, and selfishness in Judah's life?

15. Gen. 45:1-5; 50:15,19-21 **Joseph's response** – In Joseph's mind, who was most responsible for the injustices done to him? What does his view in this matter teach us about what might be involved in "humbling ourselves"?

For the **LOOK ACTIVITY** we will use the PRIDE/HUMILITY POSSIBILITIES GRAB BAG slips. Have students write out an appropriate prayer that Joseph or his brothers could have made. Listen and give counsel to sharpen the possibilities for the prayers.

At an appropriate point ask the following question to make the exercise more relevant to the student's daily lives. "Can you think of any situations that might come up at school that could be like the "Joseph's situation" you drew from the hat?" Challenge the students to write out what might be an appropriate prayer for that person and or situation. (no wrong answers, but some might need to be tweaked)

For this lesson's **TOOK ACTIVITY** we will transition to how important it is to recognize that God is sovereign and how important it is to reject pride, and embrace humility. The perfect illustration of this is found in the story of Nebuchadnezzar from Daniel 4:1-6,27-37. Review those Scriptures as an example of God warning Nebuchadnezzar to avoid pride, his falling into pride a year later, and God humbling him because he wouldn't humble himself. In the end Nebuchadnezzar properly exalts God. If only he had chosen to do that before God needed to step in. Let's avoid his failure by writing out our own version of the greatness and sovereignty of God. In other words, let's do a rewrite of Nebuchadnezzar's exaltation of God. Ask for volunteers who might be willing to read their cards while others follow it as an example of an exalting prayer.

Ask the students if they would be willing to take that home and read it every day this week as a prayer exalting God.

At some point in the lesson you might choose to ask the following questions from the short story homework: "How did pride or humility work its way out in Mr. Williams' life?" "How did pride or humility work its way out in Carla Gifford's life?" "What was the end result of these character qualities in each person's life?"

ADVANCE PREPARATION: Tell the students that the short stories of Searching for Paradise 1 & 2 will be an important part of the next lesson. Some of the next class session will involve discussion that might flow from these stories. While these stories are longer than most of the homework assignments, they will likely find them engaging and interesting to read.

Memory Verse: 2 Chronicles 7:14 if My people who are called by My name will humble themselves, and pray and seek My face, and turn from their wicked ways, then I will hear from heaven, and will forgive their sin and heal their land. NKJV

SESSION PLANNING SHEET

Session Title: __Humility___Its not all about you._____ Date: _____

Session Focus: _The character quality of humility is a vital part of prayer and God's kingdom being established on earth. _

Session Aims: **KNOW** _ that pride and humility are choices made over time in the crucible of life's challenges._____

FEEL _ that humility is a choice that will reap positive benefits and that the converse is also true._____

DO _ Write out a prayer that exalts God and read it each day this coming week._____

Session Plan	Session Activities	Preparation
Time:__15min__ APPROACH	**Methods, Instructions, Questions** **Everyone in the class take a "selfie."** **Tell the person next to you what you see? Do you agree?** **If Jesus had a cell phone camera, what would His "selfie" look like?** **2 Chronicles 7:14** if my people, who are called by my name, will humble themselves and pray and seek my face and turn from their wicked ways, then I will hear from heaven, and I will forgive their sin and will heal their land. **James 4:10** Humble ourselves **How do we do that?**	**Materials** If there is a student that doesn't have a cell phone capable of taking a selfie, offer to share yours, or have students share cell phones capable of taking a selfie
Time:__20 min__ BIBLE EXPLORATION	**Example of Joseph and his family Various passages from Genesis** **Use the Pride Humility Possibilities Grab bag for situation slips. Highlights:** Gen. 37:3,4 **Coat of many colors** Gen. 37-5-11 **Joseph's dreams** Gen. 37:18-21 **Rueben rescues him** Gen. 37:23-26 **Judah's profit scheme** Gen 37:27-28 **Joseph sold as slave** Gen. 37:29-34 **Rueben's cover up** Gen. 39:1-6 **Joseph's skill recognized** Gen. 39:7-20 **Joseph falsely accused** Gen. 39-21-23 **Joseph in charge** Gen. 41:14-16;33-41 **Joseph 2nd Egypt** Gen. 42:1-8;17 **Brothers bow down** Gen. 42:18-24 **Simeon put in jail** Gen. 43:26-34 **Benjamin honored** Gen. 44:16-18;32-34 **Judah's recompense** Gen. 45:1-5; 50:15;19-21 **Joseph's response**	Bibles Pens or pencils Student Personal Study Guides (key discussion questions)
Time:__15 min___ LIFE IMPLICATIONS	**Use the Pride Humility Possibilities Grab Bag slips.** Have the learners take the Scriptures, and have them write out an appropriate prayer that some of the family members could have made. Listen and give counsel to sharpen the possibilities for the prayers. Can you think of any situations that might come up at school that could be like the "Joseph situation" you drew from the hat? For the situation slips that you drew, write out what an appropriate prayer might have been for that person from the school.	Box or hat Pens or Pencils 3 x 5 index cards Pride/Humility Possibilities Grab bag slips
Time:__10 min__ APPLICATION	**Additional focus: The example of Nebuchadnezzar Daniel chapter 4** Do a rewrite of Nebuchadnezzar's exaltation of God. Have volunteers who are willing read their cards. Suggest that the others follow it as an example of an exalting prayer. Would you be willing to take that home and read it every day this week as a prayer exalting God? **ONE OF THE BEST WAYS TO HELP IS TO PRAY FOR THOSE IN NEED…** **Group Prayer:** Take personal prayer requests and have students pray for each other.	Slips of Joseph & his family situation scriptures Pens or Pencils 3 x 5 index cards

Session Planning Sheet ©2013 Dale Roy Erickson, adapted from material found in *Creative Bible Teaching* © 1998 by Lawrence O. Richards and Gary J. Bredfeldt, Moody Publishers. Used by permission.

Unit Four– Your Kingdom Come – Lesson 14 Humility…Prompts

There is more value in training someone to pray than to preach. It is an extraordinary challenge. It is as difficult as training a person to be an exceptional second chair violinist.   Most of us know the reason. The inspiration, effort and skill required for the task doesn't bring the desired human attention.

1 Timothy 2:1 I urge, then, first of all, that requests, prayers, intercession and thanksgiving be made for everyone   NIV

Humility is a foundational building block in our walk with God. It's not elusive, just unsought. Humble yourself. If you don't, there will always be someone who will help you with that.

James 4:10 Humble yourselves in the presence of the Lord, and He will exalt you.   NKJV

The beauty of prayer done in secret is that there really is no danger of trying to impress someone.

Matthew 6:6 But you, when you pray, go into your room, and when you have shut your door, pray to your Father who is in the secret place; and your Father who sees in secret will reward you openly.   NKJV
Proverbs 29:25 The fear of man brings a snare, But, whoever trusts in the Lord shall be safe.   NKJV

Desperate people know how to plead for mercy. They might be the only ones humble enough to do so. Our situation truly is desperate. We will only comprehend that when we see God for who He is, and ourselves as we really are.

Daniel 9:3-5 So I turned to the Lord God and pleaded with him in prayer and petition, in fasting, and in sackcloth and ashes. I prayed to the LORD my God and confessed: "O Lord, the great and awesome God, who keeps his covenant of love with all who love him and obey his commands, we have sinned and done wrong. We have been wicked and have rebelled; we have turned away from your commands and laws.   NIV

A proud and unyielding heart will find limited access to the throne of God

1 Peter 5:5 Likewise you, younger people, submit yourselves to your elders. Yes, all of you be submissive to one another, and be clothed with humility, for "God resists the proud, but gives grace to the humble."   NKJV
Luke 1:51 His mighty arm does tremendous things! How he scatters the proud and haughty ones!   NLT

We complain about the state of our culture, our country, and leadership. Do we pray about our concerns? Maybe the present state of affairs is a reflection of the present state of our prayers.

2 Chronicles 7:14 if My people who are called by My name will humble themselves, and pray and seek My face, and turn from their wicked ways, then I will hear from heaven, and will forgive their sin and heal their land.   NKJV

Here's a great test of group dynamics. Enter an unknown group and listen and watch. Take note of those who seem to be humble. Take note of those who appear to be otherwise. Which ones really seem to gain a hearing? Reflect upon what you observe, and then go to prayer.

Psalm 10:17 O LORD, You have heard the desire of the humble; You will strengthen their heart, You will incline Your ear   NKJV

Lesson Fifteen: Grace

Lesson Fifteen is the third of five lessons which will focus on kingdom qualities that are important in our prayer lives. Unit Four is called Your Kingdom Come. We will look primarily at two passages that have implications about grace. One in the Old Testament…Genesis 6:5-9,7:1; and one in the New Testament…Galatians 3:1-6. Grace is a critical concept in the Christian life and a foundational element of coming to God in prayer. It is not only the starting point of our relationship with God, but is vital in living out that relationship with God and others. There are a great variety of ways that the concept of grace is taught within the Christian faith. It will be assumed that each teacher will bring an element of their theological position regarding the underpinnings of grace. With that thought in mind, we have crafted the material in the student manual to raise a variety of issues that are often addressed when teaching about grace. The banner question used to challenge the students is: "Did grace purse them, or did they pursue grace?" The introduction to this exercise suggests that a plausible case could be made for either position. This is designed to challenge the students to give serious thought into God's desire to pursue them (by His grace) and our need to respond (i.e. pursue God's grace). Theologically speaking, this basically digs a ditch which most students (and even some of the teachers) may find difficult to fill. It is assumed that many of those who teach this curriculum will fill in that ditch from their particular point of view. It is also understood that some of our teachers will not have the theological training that would help them with this challenge. With those presuppositions, the author will throughout this lesson share his point of view. That is what authors do, you know. Centuries ago Christians killed one another over the differing points of view on this topic. Let's try to stay away from that? ☺☺ Nonetheless, we cannot do as Hebrews 4:16 ₙₖⱼᵥ instructs us: "Let us therefore come boldly to the throne of grace, that we may obtain mercy and find grace to help in time of need. ₙₖⱼᵥ" without a basic understanding of grace. We need to come boldly. We need mercy and grace. We have times of need. Perhaps before we bring our prayers before God's throne, we should find out a little more about grace.

In the **HOOK ACTIVITY** for this lesson we will use pre-wrapped gifts. Inside one of the gifts (or several if you can find willing donors) there will be a gift card. Cover the wrapped gifts with a cover of some kind. Ask for volunteers. As they volunteer, assign them numbers. First volunteer #1, second volunteer #2, etc. Uncover the gifts and tell them they have 15 seconds to find the gift card that is inside one of the wrapped gifts. Go through the numbers until the gift card is found. Ask the students how it felt to not have the opportunity to participate in the search for the gift card. Ask how it felt to search, and not find the gift. Ask how it felt to be in line to un-wrap the gift, but have someone else find the gift card first.

Transition to the **BOOK ACTIVITY** by saying that we are going to learn about the "gift of grace" and how that comes into our lives in today's lesson. Ask for a volunteer to read Genesis 6:5-9 and chapter 7 verse 1. The students who did their homework will already be familiar with this story, but for those that didn't you might want to recap Noah's story. **We are going to look at three great men of faith who accepted and un-packed their gift of grace.**

Ask for a volunteer to read Genesis 6:5-9,7:1

#1 <u>Noah</u> found grace in the eyes of the Lord. As part of this gift of grace, Noah was asked to spend 100 years building a rescue boat for his family. What would have happened if Noah and his family accepted God's grace, but didn't build the ark? According to Genesis 6:5-9,7:1, Noah's family fully accepted and un-packed their gift of grace.

Ask for a volunteer to read Galatians 3:1-6, and another volunteer to read James 2:14-21. These scriptures teach us that our experiencing of God's grace begins with a step of faith, but continues (is lived out) through a faith relationship as well.

#2 Was **Abraham** declared to be righteous because of his faith? Yes! Was Abraham's faith demonstrated and made complete by his willingness to walk out his faith through his actions? Yes ! Abraham fully accepted and un-packed his gift of grace.

Ask for a volunteer to read Acts 9:1-8 and 9:17-22. These Scriptures teach us that our experiencing of God's grace begins with God pursuing us, but continues (is lived out) through steps of obedience.

 # 3 <u>Saul</u> experienced a Supernatural encounter (as a gift of grace). Immediately following that experience, Saul was filled with the Holy Spirit, was baptized and began to preach the fact that Jesus as indeed the Messiah. Acts 9:1-8,17-22; shows us that Saul fully accepted and un-packed the gift of grace.

Transition to the **LOOK ACTIVITY** by suggesting that these men are just three of many who have found that God pursued them with His gift of grace. They chose to respond positively to God's offer, and then realized the full effect. In other words, they actually lived out the grace relationship that God desired for them. Let's look at how these elements can be found in their relationship with God. If the majority of students in your group come with their homework done, you can make this a discussion of what they put on the "Grace found them or they found grace" exercise. If the majority of your group doesn't come with their homework completed, you will have to use time in class to have the students prepare their responses.

Adam & Eve - Genesis 3:16-19 Did grace pursue them, or did they pursue grace? Clearly God pursued them with His grace as evidenced by the fact that their sin didn't cost them their physical lives. The relationship with God continued. What are the possible implications of that? On the other hand, there were clear consequences for their sin which grace did not revoke (cover). They were kicked out of the garden of Eden, kept away from the tree of life, the ground was cursed, birth was accompanied with pain, etc. Their relationship with God's created world changed. What are the possible implications of that?

Noah - Genesis 6:5-9 Did grace pursue him, or did he pursue grace? God's grace clearly pursued Noah, and God intervened by inviting Noah and his family to build their rescue boat. What are the possible implications of that?

Noah pursued grace by taking 100 years to build his rescue boat.
What are the possible implications of that?

Abraham - Romans 4:1-8 Did grace pursue him, or did he pursue grace? God's grace reached out to Abraham by calling him away from his family and taking him to a new land of promise. What are the possible implications of that?

Abraham pursued grace by responding with faith and obedience into the land of promise even to the point of giving up his miracle child son (promised heir). What are the possible implications of that?

Israelites in Egypt - Exodus 3:7-10 Did grace pursue them, or did they pursue grace? God reached out to the Israelites in Egypt by sending Moses as a deliverer and performing a miraculous plan of escape. What are the possible implications of that?

The Israelites pursued grace by crying out for God to intervene and deliver them from slavery. What are the possible implications of that?

Rahab Joshua 2:3-14 Did grace pursue her, or did she pursue grace? God pursued grace for Rahab by providing a means of escape from destruction for her and her family. What are the possible implications of that?

Rahab pursued grace by believing that the God of Israel was powerful enough to destroy Jericho. She protected the Israeli spies and asked for protection when destruction came. What are the possible implications of that?

Jonah & Ninevites – Jonah 1:14; 2:2,10; 3:6-10; 4:2,11 Did grace pursue them, or did they pursue grace? When God pursued the Ninevites with His grace, Jonah didn't want to bring the message of grace. God refused to let Jonah run way from delivering the message of coming judgment for sin. What are the possible implications of that?

The Ninevites pursued grace with fasting and repentance, and God forestalled their judgment. What are the possible implications of that?

Hosea – Hosea 2:1-4; 14:1-9 Did grace pursue them, or did they pursue grace? In spite of their unfaithfulness, God pursues the nation of Israel because of His loving-kindness and compassion. What are the possible implications of that?

The end of Hosea has God calling for them to repent, and promises to forgive them and heal them. What are the possible implications of that?

Prodigal Son – Luke 15:11-14; 20-24 Did grace pursue him, or did he pursue grace? The father in the Prodigal Son story didn't pursue the son to a foreign country, but he did keep watching for his return. His watchfulness reflects a readiness to extend grace, and the welcome home reflects the full application of that grace. The prodigal walked away from the relationship with his father, and as long as he stayed away the father's grace had little impact. What are the possible implications of that?

When the prodigal chose to return, the grace of the father was quickly and fully (even beyond expectation) realized and the relationship was restored. What are the possible implications of that? The older brother struggled to extend the same grace and restored relationship. What are the possible implications of that?

Thief on the cross – Luke 23:39-43 Did grace pursue him, or did he pursue grace? Jesus clearly, through his actions and the dialogue with the thieves on the cross, was extending (making possible) His grace. What are the possible implications of that?

One of the thieves pursued grace by asking for it (and thus receiving grace), while the other thief apparently didn't ask for grace. What are the possible implications of that?

Peter after resurrection – Mark 14:27-31,70-72; John 21:15-19 Did grace pursue him, or did he pursue grace? Jesus told the women who first saw him resurrected: "Go tell the disciples and Peter" that I will meet them in Galilee. By referencing Peter by name, Jesus could have been sending a signal that Peter was forgiven for his untimely denials of knowing Jesus. What are the possible implications of that?

After denying Jesus, Peter went out and wept, which was probably a signal of repentance. When Jesus saw Peter in Galilee shortly thereafter, he asked him 3 times if he loved him. Peter's answers and Jesus' prediction reflect the restored nature of their relationship. What are the possible implications of that?

Paul on the road to Damascus – Acts 9:1-8,13-16,20 Did grace pursue him, or did he pursue grace? Clearly Jesus stopped him with a blinding light. He had been persecuting the followers of Christ. Jesus told Ananias that Paul was a chosen instrument who would bear His name before the Gentiles and kings and the sons of Israel. He would also suffer in Jesus name. He responded by immediately beginning to proclaim that Jesus was the "the Son of God."

The key questions for this activity would be found in their answers to these two questions:

How about you? Give a summary statement about the way "grace pursued you." _____

_____

_____

How about you? Give a summary statement about how "you have pursued grace." _____

_____

_____

_____

Each of the people we have looked at today had their lives significantly changed by God's gift of grace. They each entered into a new relationship with God that found expression in how they lived the rest of their lives.

For the **TOOK ACTIVITY** let's take a moment and ask God how we can "un-pack" the gift of grace in our lives. One of the ways is to connect with God on a daily basis through prayer. Hebrews 4:16 says that we can come boldly before the throne of grace to obtain mercy and help in times of trouble. That applies not only for ourselves, but also for others as well. Let's pray that God's grace reaches those we love with salvation and helps them in times of trouble.

Take personal prayer requests and have students pray for each other.

We have been studying the Lord's Prayer for some time now. Right now, we are focused on how God desires to bring His kingdom into our lives. In Jesus' words: "your kingdom come, your will be done on earth as it is in heaven." Grace is the only means of entry into God's heavenly kingdom. Our eternal existence will have grace at its very core. On earth, grace is meant to be the channel (life expression) of His Kingdom. Our Christian life (including our prayers) begins with embracing the grace of our Lord, and finds expression through a grace filled life.

Memory Verse: Titus 2:11,12 For the grace of God has appeared, bringing salvation for all people, training us to renounce ungodliness and worldly passions, and to live self-controlled, upright, and godly lives in the present age. NKJV

SESSION PLANNING SHEET

Session Title: __Finding Grace and Grace Finding You_____ Date: _____

Session Focus: _The gift of grace must be accepted, embraced, and expressed in order to be fulfilled in the Christian life.__

Session Aims: **KNOW** _ Acknowledge that a gift is of very little value until it is opened and received._____

   FEEL _ Express the joy found in un-packing a gift, and discovering something of genuine value._____

   DO _ Discover the full value of a gift by taking it to the place where it can be redeemed._____

Session Plan	Session Activities	Preparation
Time:__15min__ APPROACH	**Methods, Instructions, Questions** **Un-packing your gift.** **Volunteers by number according to how quickly they volunteered.** 15 seconds to open gifts and search for something worthwhile. How did it feel to be the one who found the gift card? How did it feel to search and not be the one who found it? How did it feel to sit on the sidelines while they searched? **Compare to those who search for God in the wrong places.**	**Materials** Wrap many gifts of different sizes with packing peanuts inside. Place redeemable gift card or coupons inside the gifts.
Time:__20 min__ BIBLE EXPLORATION	These great men of faith accepted and un-packed their gift of grace. **Noah** found grace in the eyes of the Lord. What would have happened if Noah and his family accepted God's grace, but didn't build the ark? Noah's family fully un-packed their gift of grace. Genesis 6:5-9,7:1 Was **Abraham** declared to be righteous because of his faith? Gal. 3:1-6 Yes. Was Abraham's faith demonstrated and made complete by his willingness to walk out his faith through his actions? James 2:14-21 Yes. Abraham fully accepted and un-packed his gift of grace. **Saul** experienced a Supernatural encounter (as a gift of grace). Acts 9:1-8; 9:17-22 Saul fully accepted and un-packed the gift of grace.	Bibles Student Participation Study Guides Pens or pencils
Time:__15 min___ LIFE IMPLICATIONS	**How did grace pursue the following people? How did they pursue grace?** Adam and Eve – Genesis 3:16-19 Noah – Genesis 6:5-9 Abraham – Romans 4:1-8 Israelites in Egypt – Exodus 3:7-10 Rahab – Joshua 2:3-14 Hosea – Hosea 2:1-4; 14:1-9 Jonah & Ninevites – Jonah 1:14; 2:2,10; 3:6-10; 4:2,11 Prodigal Son – Luke 15-11-14; 20-24 Thief on the cross – Luke 23:39-43 Peter after resurrection – Mark 14:27-31,70-72; John 21:15-19 Paul on the road to Damascus – Acts 9:1-8,13-16,20 **How about you? How has God's gift of grace pursued you? Since you first discovered His grace, how have you un-packed this great gift?**	
Time:__10 min__ APPLICATION	Each of the people we have looked at today had their lives significantly changed by God's gift of grace. They each entered into a new relationship with God that found expression in how they lived the rest of their lives. Let's take a moment, and ask God how we can "un-pack" the gift of grace in our lives. One of the ways is to connect with God on a daily basis through prayer. **Take personal prayer requests and have students pray for each other.**	

Session Planning Sheet ©2013 Dale Roy Erickson, adapted from material found in *Creative Bible Teaching* © 1998 by Lawrence O. Richards and Gary J. Bredfeldt, Moody Publishers. Used by permission.

Unit Three – Your Kingdom Come – Lesson 15 Grace…Prompts

When we come before God in prayer, we must understand that we are approaching the throne of grace. Grace and grace alone provides access and is the foundation for our requests.

Hebrews 4:16 Therefore let us draw near with confidence to the throne of grace, so that we may receive mercy and find grace to help in time of need. ₙₐₛв

Grace is available for everyone, but only received by those who recognize their need for it and the source of supply.

Romans 3:23,24 for all have sinned and fall short of the glory of God, being justified as a gift by His grace through the redemption which is in Christ Jesus ₙₐₛв **Acts 17:30-31** "Therefore having overlooked the times of ignorance, God is now declaring to men that all *people* everywhere should repent, because He has fixed a day in which He will judge the world in righteousness through a Man whom He has appointed, having furnished proof to all men by raising Him from the dead." ₙₐₛв

While we cannot "earn" grace, there are some heart conditions that will restrict our access to God's grace. In fact, when we will allow our hearts to be filled with pride, we may find resistance from God instead of grace.

1 Peter 5:5 Likewise you younger people, submit yourselves to *your* elders. Yes, all of *you* be submissive to one another, and be clothed with humility, for "**God resists the proud**, but gives grace to **the humble**." ₙₗт

Many people view "grace" like the atmosphere. Once we walk into God's grace it surrounds us like the air we breathe. Perhaps we should think of it more like a garden that we have to grow. Perhaps we should prepare the soil, properly set the plants, keep the weeds out, water it regularly, and always leave room for the plants to reach for the heavens.

2 Peter 3:18 but grow in the grace and knowledge of our Lord and Savior Jesus Christ. To Him *be* the glory both now and forever. Amen. **Romans 6:1-2** What shall we say then? Shall we continue in sin that grace may abound? Certainly not! How shall we who died to sin live any longer in it? ₙₖⱼᵥ

We don't earn grace by our good behavior. We accept it.

Ephesians 2:8-10 God saved you by his grace when you believed. And you can't take credit for this; it is a gift from God. ⁹ Salvation is not a reward for the good things we have done, so none of us can boast about it. ¹⁰ For we are God's masterpiece. He has created us anew in Christ Jesus, so we can do the good things he planned for us long ago. ₙₗт

If you want to enter the royal court or the Oval office, you may need an introduction. Our access into the grace in which we stand is Jesus Christ our Redeemer.

Romans 5:2 through whom also we have obtained our introduction by faith into this grace in which we stand; and we exult in hope of the glory of God. ₙₐₛв

God is not stingy with His grace. He is happy to give generously to those with the right attitude.

James 4:6 And he gives grace generously. As the Scriptures say, "God opposes the proud, but gives grace to the humble." ₙₗт

God's nature of love and kindness is the driving force behind our standing with God. It is clearly His work in us, not our work for Him.

Titus 3:4-6 But when the kindness of God our Savior and *His* love for mankind appeared, ⁵ He saved us, not on the basis of deeds which we have done in righteousness, but according to His mercy, by the washing of regeneration and renewing by the Holy Spirit, ⁶ whom He poured out upon us richly through Jesus Christ our Savior. ₙₐₛв

It is so easy to tell God that He has to be "fair with us"…that we deserve this or that. Our relationship with God begins with "undeserved grace" and continues with "underserved grace." Let's make sure that we keep this truth in the front of our minds as we pray.

Acts 15:11 We believe that we are all saved the same way, by the undeserved grace of the Lord Jesus. ₙₗт

Lesson Sixteen: Faith

Lesson Sixteen is the fourth of five lessons which will focus on kingdom qualities especially linked to prayer. Unit Four is called Your Kingdom come. In today's lesson we will focus on how significant faith is in our prayer life. Faith is clearly a critical factor in all of the Christian life. But for our purposes we will specifically apply it to exercising faith in our prayer life. Faith, whether in our prayers, or in the general sense has great variety in how it is taught and emphasized in Christian circles. Rather than dive into specific "hot topics" on this issue, like the faith healing or prosperity doctrine streams, we will address it in the more general sense of Biblical examples of faith. In that sense the two most poignant verses are Hebrews 11:1 and 11:6. They define what faith is, and how important it is in our relationship with God. They say: "Now faith is the substance of things hoped for, the evidence of things not seen. But without faith *it is* impossible to please *Him,* for he who comes to God must believe that He is, and *that* He is a rewarder of those who diligently seek Him." The first lays out the focus of the person of faith, and the second the expectations of God and the expectations of the person who comes in faith. These Biblical statements are succinct articulations of the topic. Reflecting on, and/or memorizing these two verses, provides a great foundation for our lesson today. In order to further build on that foundation, we will look at some of the most preeminent examples of people who walked it out in their personal experience.

For the **HOOK ACTIVITY** tell the students that you will help them memorize "word for word" a critical verse about faith in 10 minutes or less. Take a white or digital board that has the key verse of the lesson written out. Have the students recite each word on the board together. After doing that twice, erase one of the words and have the group recite it. Ask for a volunteer to recite the verses without the assistance of the rest of the group. If the volunteer recites the verse correctly, erase one more word and have the group recite it. Ask for another volunteer to recite the verse. Continue this activity until the entire group has recited Hebrews 11:6 without any words being left on the board.

When that is complete, transition to the **BOOK ACTIVITY** by saying: "We have the expectations of faith" down pat. Now, let's look at what that looks like in the lives of some people who walked that out in real life. We are going to look at what many people call the Hall of Faith chapter of the Bible…Hebrews 11. Have various students read a portion of the chapter until the entire chapter has been read out loud. Tell them that it is important for the next activity that they take a careful look at this passage. Have them read it one more time silently. Turn over the Steps of faith matching exercise. Students can then compete to see who can match the faith expression to the correct character. Warn them that two of the faith expressions sound very similar, so they will have to pay attention to the details.

STEPS OF FAITH MATCHING EXERCISE

1. __i__ Wrestled with God to obtain
   a promised blessing

   a) Judges 4:14,15 Barak

2. __f__ Hid spies for Israel

   b) Judges 7:16-22 Gideon

3. __h__ Proclaimed prophetic blessings
   to future generations on his deathbed

   c) Genesis 5:21-24 Enoch

25

4. __m__ Refused to become an Egyptian prince   d) Genesis 27:27-29, 38-40 Isaac

5. __j__ Appointed Saul to be the first king of Israel   e) Genesis 17:15-17, 21:1-7 Sarah

6. __l__ Made a better sacrifice to God than his brother   f) Joshua 2:8-14 Rahab

7. __a__ Listened to a female prophetess and won a victory g) Judges 15:1-5 Samson

8. __d__ Gave a prophetic blessing on his twin boys   h) Genesis 50:24-26 Joseph

9. __b__ Defeated an enormous army with 300 warriors   i) Genesis 32:24-30 Jacob

10. __e__ Had a baby at age 90   j) 1 Samuel 8:3-6,17-22 Samuel

11. __k__ defeated a 9' warrior with a sling   k) 1 Samuel 17:31-33, 46-50 David

12. __c__ First person to avoid physical death   l) Genesis 4:3-5 Abel

13. __g__ Set an enemy field on fire using foxes   m) Exodus 2:10-15 Moses

14. __o__ Probably spent 100 years on a faith building project n) Genesis 21:5 Abraham

15. __n__ Was 100 years old when his miracle child was born o) Genesis 5:32,7:6 Noah

If time constraints allow, give some context and additional details for the faith expressions when you share the correct answers. Next, if time permits, we will talk about God's response when our Hall of Faith characters failed to exercise faith. Tell the students that it would be more difficult to step out in faith if God rejected us when we fail. Have the students look up these events and give a short summary of what happened.

Let's look at some examples of how the people who made it to the "faith hall of fame" seemed to fail the test?

Abraham - Genesis 12:10-14; 20:1-2,10-13 _____

_____

Gideon – Judges 6:13-16,36-40 _____

_____

Barak – Judges 4:5-9 _____

_____

Sarah - Genesis 16:1-4 _____

_____

Samson - Judges 16:15-20_____

_____

Israel – 1 Samuel 8:1-8 _____

_____

David – 1 Samuel 21:1-2,10-15 _____

_____

Moses – Exodus 4:1-5,10-13 _____

_____

Let's reflect upon New Covenant leaders who at one point in their lives may have failed to step forward in faith.

Peter - Matthew 14:15-32 _____

_____

Thomas & the disciples the day after the crucifixion - Matt. 16:21-23, John 11:38-46, Mark 16:9-15

_____

_____

Church at Mary the mother of John (i.e. Mark's) house - Acts 12:5,12-15 _____

_____

TEACHER NOTES RE: THE HALL OF FAITH CHARACTERS

Abel: Why was Abel's sacrifice more acceptable than Cain's? Some believe that Abel gave a better sacrifice because he brought the "firstlings and fat portions." In other words, he brought the first and best portions. Others believe that when God provided garments of skin for clothing that it represented an animal sacrifice, and that the family knew that an animal would be a better offering to bring. Some people believe that it was Abel's heart attitude that made the offering more acceptable.

Enoch: Genesis 5 doesn't tell us that Enoch didn't die, but Hebrews 11 specifically tells us that fact.

Noah: Scripture records that Noah was 500 and became the father of Shem, Ham and Japheth. Since they were different ages, this reference makes more sense as a marker in time. At 500 he was their father. The next time marker was when the ark was completed. The family project was completed about 100 years later.

Abraham: Was 100 years old when the promised child was born to him. There were many steps of faith before that time. He left his home not knowing where he was going. He delivered Lot through repeated intercession. He also failed in several ways, including (in an act of fear rather than faith) representing his wife as his sister (actually she was step sister, but that is irrelevant) and having a child through his wife's servant (maid). He was willing to offer up Isaac believing that God would raise him back from the dead.

Sarah: She encouraged her husband to have a child by getting her servant pregnant (not an act of faith), and laughed when the angel said she would have a child at 90, but then responded in faith to God's work.

Isaac: On his deathbed he prophesied about the future of Jacob and Esau.

Jacob: On his death bed he prophesied about the future of the descendants of Joseph's sons.

Joseph: On his death bed he prophesied about the future exodus of the people of Israel, and gave instructions about his bones.

Moses: The steps of faith by this man are myriad, and include choosing to identify with the Israeli slaves rather than the nobility of Pharaoh's family, proclaiming God's judgments to Pharaoh, keeping the Passover, parting the Red Sea, and many more. In spite of seeing God turn his staff into a snake, and then back into a staff again, and seeing the burning bush, he asked God to choose someone else because he didn't speak well enough, taking judgment into his own hand by killing an Egyptian master, and striking a rock instead of speaking to it as directed by God.

Rahab: Risked her life by hiding the Israeli spies from the people of Jericho.

Gideon: After God promised to be with him, he asked for two proofs that God would help him (fleeces). He led 300 against an innumerable army and God gave them the victory.

Barak: Asked a prophetess for advice, and then would only accept her word from God if she put her life on the line to back up what she said.

Samson: God used him to accomplish many supernatural feats of strength and to bring victories over the Philistines (enemies of God's people). In a moment of weakness he revealed a secret which allowed the breaking of a vow that he had kept since birth.

Jephthah: Led a great victory for the people of Israel, but made a foolish vow in the process.

David: Had many moments of great faith, including the killing of a 9' enemy champion (Goliath) with a sling and some stones.

Peter: Peter was the quintessential example of stepping out in faith, from stepping out of the boat to walk on the water, to speaking up on Pentecost, and confronting the Jewish religious leaders. He is also a good example of those who failed in a big way. Whether it was sinking when he was walking on the water, or denying Jesus on the night before his crucifixion, Peter rode the faith rollercoaster. In the walking on water example it might be good to remind the students that on the day of that event the disciples watched Jesus turn a few loaves and fishes into enough food to feed 5000 people. It would be a good idea to remind the students of how Jesus responded to Peter after the resurrection. It was a non-judgmental response (Do you love me?) followed by a commission.

Thomas and all the disciples: In spite of being told several times before the crucifixion that Jesus would be killed and rise from the dead…Thomas and the all the disciples did not believe the ladies when told that Jesus had been raised from the dead. Thomas is the most notable example. Jesus' response to him was to present the evidence and then call him to faith.

Church at Mary the mother of John (i.e. Mark's) house: The entire church was gathered to pray for Peter's release from prison, but when Rhoda told them that Peter was at the door, they thought she was crazy. One is an example of praying in faith, and the other an example of disbelief.

Transition to the **LOOK ACTIVITY** by asking the students to review the following questions:

What was Jesus response to them? What does that tell you to expect in His response to your steps of faith?

_____

_____

What does that tell you personally about stepping out in faith in order to follow Jesus? _____

_____

_____

Make the transition to the **TOOK ACTIVITY** by asking: "What examples can you give of God clearly working on your behalf?" Big or small…they all count. Next invite them to take a few moments to silently reflect upon God's faith building examples in the lives of the biblical characters we have looked at today. Tell God what their example means to you.

Take a few moments to silently reflect upon the faith building examples in your own life and those of your friends and family. Tell God what that means to you.

Let God know if you are willing to take another step of faith. Ask Him if He might have a step of faith that He wants you to take in the coming week.

Memory Verse: Hebrews 11:6 But without faith it is impossible to please Him, for he who comes to God must believe that He is, and that He is a rewarder of those who diligently seek Him. NKJV

SESSION PLANNING SHEET

Session Title: __ Kingdom qualities - Without Faith It Is Impossible To Please God. _____ Date: _____

Session Focus: __Understanding how critical faith is in our relationship with God. _____

Session Aims: **KNOW** _Identify Biblical passages that inform us on how to come to God in genuine faith. _____

FEEL _ Express a personal confidence that with God's help you can move ahead in a step of faith. _____

DO _ Write out a potential "step of faith" that you would be willing to take this coming week. _____

Session Plan	Session Activities	Preparation
Time:__15min__ APPROACH	**Methods, Instructions, Questions** **MEMORY VERSE CHALLENGE: Hebrews 11:6** We can all memorize Hebrews 11:6 "word perfect" in 10 minutes or less. Have group say the verse together. Then ask for an individual volunteer to say the verse with one word removed from the white/digital board. If they incorrectly recite the verse, have a different volunteer share the correct response. Then remove another word and repeat process. One word is removed in each step when a random individual correctly recites the verse. Finish this exercise by having the entire group recite the verse. **Indiana Jones Faith Walk** https://www.youtube.com/watch?v=xFntFdEGgws	**Materials** White or digital board Dry erase pen White board eraser
Time:__20 min__ BIBLE EXPLORATION	**What faith looks like...What happened before the step of faith.** **Hebrews 11 Steps of Faith Matching exercise** Have students match up the Hall of Faith characters with the steps of faith that they took in their lives. Follow that up with the **Hall of Faith Slip Up** worksheet. O.T. examples: Abraham – Gen.12:10-14,20:1-2,10-13 Gideon – Judges 6:13-16, 36-40 Barak – Judges 4:5-9 Sarah - Genesis 16:1-4 Samson - Judges 16:15-20 Israel – 1 Samuel 8:1-8 David – 1 Samuel 21:1-2,10-15 Moses – Exodus 4:1-5,10-13 N.T. examples: Peter - Matthew 14:15-27 Disciples – Matt. 16:21-23, John 11:38-46, Mark 16:9-15 Church at Mary's house – Acts 12:5,12-15, Saul Acts 7:57-8:3, 9:1-2	Steps of Faith Matching Worksheets, Bible, Pens Hall of Faith Slip Up Worksheets, Bibles, Pens
Time:__15 min___ LIFE IMPLICATIONS	**Two Questions Review** What was Jesus' response to them? What does that tell you to expect in His response to your steps of faith? What does that tell you personally about stepping out in faith in order to follow Jesus? What examples can you give of God clearly working on your behalf? Big or small...they all count.	
Time:__10 min__ APPLICATION	Take a few moments to silently reflect upon God's faith building examples in the lives of the biblical characters we have looked at today. Tell God what their example means to you. Take a few moments to silently reflect upon the faith building examples in your own life and those of your friends and family. Tell God what that means to you. Let God know if you are willing to take another step of faith if and when He asks you to step out in faith. Ask Him if He has something He would like you to step out in faith about in the coming week. **ONE OF THE BEST WAYS TO HELP IS TO PRAY FOR THOSE IN NEED...**	

Session Planning Sheet ©2013 Dale Roy Erickson, adapted from material found in *Creative Bible Teaching* © 1998 by Lawrence O. Richards and Gary J. Bredfeldt, Moody Publishers. Used by permission.

Unit Four – Your Kingdom Come – Lesson 16 Faith...Prompts

Down through the ages the great men and women of the Christian faith have indicated that the world is changed through God's response to the prayers of His people. You might think: "That's fine for them, but I'm no saint....my prayers will never be world changing." You are right. "You" can't, but He can!

Isaiah 64:4 Since ancient times no one has heard, no ear has perceived, no eye has seen any God besides you, who acts on behalf of those who wait for him. NIV

The impact of our lives will have three limiting factors. They are the size of our (God given) dreams, the size of our (God given) faith, and our view of the greatness of our God.

Matthew 17:20 And He said to them, "Because of the littleness of your faith; for truly I say to you, if you have faith the size of a mustard seed, you will say to this mountain, 'Move from here to there,' and it will move; and nothing will be impossible to you. NIV

God clearly calls us to pray in faith without doubting, but what is His response to faith that needs to grow?

Luke 9:23,24,27 And Jesus said to him, " 'If You can?' All things are possible to him who believes." Immediately the boy's father cried out and said, "I do believe; help my unbelief." But Jesus took him by the hand and raised him; and he got up. NASB

Acts 12:15,16 They said to her, "You are out of your mind!" But she kept insisting that it was so. They kept saying, "It is his angel." But Peter continued knocking; and when they had opened the door, they saw him and were amazed. NASB

Prayer is the first and best expression of where our confidence lies. Faith and works will find expression both in and when we leave our secret place with God.

1 John 5:14,15 Now this is the confidence that we have in Him, that if we ask anything according to His will, He hears us. And if we know that He hears us, whatever we ask, we know that we have the petitions that we have asked of Him NKJV

There are times when a 5-year-old may not understand what their parents are doing. They might even have their own view of how things should be done. A good parent is willing to listen, to explain what is happening to the best of the child's ability to understand, and then ask the child to trust them. Oh...to have the faith of a child.

John 11:21-23 Martha then said to Jesus, "Lord, if You had been here, my brother would not have died. "Even now I know that whatever You ask of God, God will give You." Jesus said to her, "Your brother will rise again." NASB

Prayer begins and ends in our hearts. It pleases Him that we come in faith, believing in Him and that He will reward us for coming.

Hebrews 11:6 But without faith it is impossible to please Him, for he who comes to God must believe that He is, and that He is a rewarder of those who diligently seek Him. NKJV

What measure do we use to determine a person's value? We often use power, wealth, accomplishments, and the approval of others as standards. The true measure of a man or woman is determined by their faith in God.

Matthew 9:29 Then He touched their eyes, saying, "It shall be done to you according to your faith." NASB

Lesson Seventeen: Joy

Lesson Seventeen is the fifth of five lessons which will focus on kingdom qualities especially linked to prayer. Unit Four is called Your Kingdom come. In today's lesson we will focus on how significant joy is in our Christian life. David said in Psalm 16:11 NKJV *"In your presence is fullness of joy. At your right hand are pleasures forevermore."* In other words, being in His presence should bring joy to our lives. Yes, we will bring our sorrows, our requests and struggles, but ultimately being in His presence should bring us joy. The consummate expression of this will be when we have left this earthly domain. In some respects, even now, our times of prayer should transport us beyond our normal human experience. God speaks of this truth when addressing His people in Isaiah 56:7 NLT *"I will bring them to my holy mountain of Jerusalem and will fill them with joy in my house of prayer."* The Bible has a lot more to say about God wanting to bring joy into our lives. We are going to take a look at that in today's lesson.

For the **HOOK ACTIVITY** we will take a more general look at what the Bible has to say about joy in the Christian life. The Bible Project has a 4-minute video that gives a concise overview of this topic. At the start, it is a little too focused on the etymology of the word "joy" for our typical HOOK purposes. Once the video moves past this element, it accomplishes the goals we have for this part of the lesson. You can find this video on YouTube at: **https://www.youtube.com/watch?v=qvOhQTuD2e0.** It can also be found at: **www.thebibleproject.com.** Look for the Advent Series and find the "Chara: Joy" video. This video highlights the concept that Biblical joy involves choosing to look past our present circumstances to our ultimate destination. It is God's intention that we live an abundant life and that "life and/or joy" will be found in our relationship with Him. We know that there are challenges or distractions that can steal away our joy. Transition to the **BOOK ACTIVITY** by saying, "Let's look together at a good example of this from Luke 15." In this example, we will ask you to see the role of the father as representing our relationship with God the Father. What possible challenges or distractions did these people face that kept them from restoring their relationship with God? What was the result when the situation was resolved?

If your setting would respond better to a more lighthearted start to this lesson, you might consider an **ALTERNATE** hook activity. You might use the following Spoof of Prince Andrew and Kate's wedding. You will find it on YouTube at: **https://www.youtube.com/watch?v=Kav0FEhtLug**. Introduce the video by suggesting that the British people are known throughout the world for their ability to organize very dignified ceremonies. You can connect this video to the recent wedding of Prince Harry. Ask how many of the students saw some of the elements of his wedding. Suggest in today's lesson we will learn about the significance of how royalty and nobility are treated in public. Once they have seen the video, ask them what was wrong with what happened. Ask them what could be right about what happened. Can they picture the God that we correctly approach with reverence and awe ever celebrating or expressing joy in an unconstrained manner? Transition to the BOOK ACTIVITY by saying, "Let's look together at a good example of this from Luke 15." In this example, emphasize that all of heaven rejoices when one sinner is restored in their relationship with God. Ask them to come up with some possible challenges or distractions that kept them from restoring their relationship with God? What was the result when the situation was resolved?

What were some of the challenges or distractions the <u>shepherd</u> might have faced? The biggest one that is inferred in this parable is the idea that he must focus on the 99 sheep instead of the 1 that was lost. Any number of other things to focus on will be acceptable answers.

What was the result when the situation was resolved? The shepherd placed the lost sheep on his shoulders and invites everyone to come together for a time of rejoicing. One of the greatest reasons to rejoice can be over someone repenting, and being restored in their relationship with God.

What were some of the challenges or distractions the <u>woman</u> might have faced? Her attention could have been drawn away to other concerns, like her children, her other work, or securing a safe place for the coins she still had. Any number of other things to focus on will be acceptable answers.

What was the result when the situation was resolved? She gathered friends and family for a time of rejoicing.

What were some of the distractions the <u>younger brother</u> might have faced? Many of them are listed in the parable, and most could be reflected in the phrase: "wine, women and song." It is very easy for teens to supplant important family relationships with their friends and other distractions. At a certain point mere survival was the challenge he was facing, and then he came to his senses.

What was the result when the situation was resolved? He was reunited with his father and a celebration ensued.

What were some of the challenges or distractions the <u>older brother</u> might have faced? Running the family business was a challenge and a distraction that influenced the family relationships. The older brother minimized the importance of the relationships within the family. He cast aspersions (accusations) on his brother rather than rejoicing in his return.

What was the result when the situation was resolved? The father (representing God in this case) kept the focus on celebrating (rejoicing) in the restored relationships. We don't really know if the brother joined the celebration, but clearly the challenge is to rejoice in people returning to the Father.

Which of those distractions would <u>you</u> find most challenging? There will be no wrong answer in this part of the lesson. Depending on how close knit your group or setting has become, you may need to make this a silent personal reflection question.

What will be the result when your situation is resolved? There will be no wrong answer in this part of the lesson. Depending on how close knit your group or setting has become, you may need to make this a silent personal reflection question.

Here are the answers to the fill in the blank spaces exercise from the Student Personal Study Guide. When the students have completed the exercise, have them place the Scripture reference in one of the three columns listed in the **Where Joy Come From** table. You will need four different versions of the Bible for this exercise. Be certain that they are available for this activity. You might want to divide the group into teams of 4 (1 for each translation) and have them look up the verses and share the answers with one another. In some settings, the internet may be a substitute for actually bringing the four translations.

Isaiah 12:2-3 _{NASB} Behold, God is my **salvation**, I will **trust** and not be **afraid**; For the LORD GOD is my **strength** and **song**, And He has become my **salvation**." Therefore, you will **joyously** draw **water** from the **springs** of salvation.

Nehemiah 12:43 _{NLT} Many sacrifices were offered on that **joyous** day, for God had given the people cause for **great joy**. The women and children also **participated** in the **celebration**, and the **joy** of the people of Jerusalem could be heard far away.

Galatians 5:22-23 _{NLT} But the **Holy Spirit** produces this kind of **fruit** in our lives: love, **joy**, peace, **patience**, kindness, goodness, faithfulness, **gentleness**, and self-control. There is no law against these things!

Romans 15:13 _{NASB} Now may the God of hope fill you with all **joy** and **peace** in believing, so that you will abound in **hope** by the **power** of the Holy Spirit.

Jeremiah 31:12 _{NLT} They will come home and sing **songs** of **joy** on the heights of Jerusalem. They will be **radiant** because of the LORD's good **gifts**—the **abundant** crops of grain, new wine, and olive oil, and the **healthy** flocks and herds. Their **life** will be like a watered garden, and all their **sorrows** will be gone.

Psalm 4:7 _{NLT} You have given me **greater joy** than those who have **abundant** harvests of **grain** and new **wine**.

Philippians 1:4 _{NASB} Always offering **prayer** with **joy** in my every **prayer** for you all.

Isaiah 56:7 _{NASB} Even those I will bring to My holy mountain And make them **joyful** in My house of **prayer**. Their burnt offerings and their sacrifices will be **acceptable** on My altar; For My house will be called a house of **prayer** for all the peoples."

Acts 13:52 _{NKJV} And the disciples were **filled** with **joy** and with the **Holy Spirit**. **Luke 1:46-49** _{NKJV} And Mary said: "My soul **magnifies** the Lord, and my spirit has **rejoiced** in God my Savior. For He has regarded the lowly state of His maidservant; for behold, henceforth all generations will call me **blessed**. For He who is mighty has done **great things** for me, and holy *is* His name.

Psalm 28:7 _{NIV} The Lord is my **strength** and my **shield**; my heart **trusts** in him, and he **helps** me. My **heart** leaps for **joy**, and with my song I **praise** him.

Philippians 3:1 _{NLT} **Whatever** happens, my dear brothers and sisters, **rejoice** in the Lord. I never get tired of telling you these things, and I do it to **safeguard** your faith.

Luke 24:52,53 _{NLT} They **worshiped** him and then returned to Jerusalem **filled** with **great joy**. And they spent all of their time in the Temple, **praising** God.

Psalms 16:11 _{NASB} You will make known to me the **path** of life; In Your **presence** is **fullness** of **joy**; In Your **right** hand there are **pleasures** forever.

2 Chronicles 6:41 _{NASB} Now therefore arise, O LORD God, to Your resting place, You and the ark of Your might; let Your priests, O LORD God, be clothed with **salvation** and let Your godly ones **rejoice** in what is **good**.

Philippians 4:4 _{NLT} **Always** be **full** of **joy** in the Lord. I say it again--**rejoice**!

Psalm 21:6 _{NIV} Surely you have granted him **unending blessings** and made him **glad** with the **joy** of your **presence**.

Psalm 43:4 _{NLT} There I will go to the altar of God, to God--the **source** of all my **joy**. I will **praise** you with my harp, O God, my God!

Philippians 2:18 _{NASB} You too, I urge you, **rejoice** in the same way and **share** your **joy** with me

Isaiah 9:3 _{NKJV} You have multiplied the nation and **increased** its **joy**; They **rejoice** before You according to the **joy** of **harvest**, as men rejoice when they divide the **spoil**.

Some of the references may fit into more than one category.

Where joy comes from		
Joy is a gift	Joy is a choice	Joy in response to God's goodness
Galatians 5:22-23	Isaiah 12:2-3	Nehemiah 12:43
Romans 15:13	Philippians 1:4	Jeremiah 31:12
Psalms 4:7	Psalms 28:7	Luke 1:46-49
Isaiah 56:7	Philippians 3:1	Psalms 16:11
Acts 13:52	2 Chronicles 6:41	Psalms 43:4
Luke 24:52-53	Philippians 4:4	Isaiah 9:3
Psalms 21:6	Philippians 2:18	

For the **LOOK** Activity we will review the way we can find joy in unusual places in our everyday life. Using the characters in the short story, "A Closer Walk," find some examples of overlooked sources of joy. Write down what you have found.

Sandy She found joy in roaming the hills with her brother, in singing her favorite hymn, the warmth of the sun and her brother's windbreaker, in Mr. Hemstreet's smile, and a beautiful Christmas tree.

Blake He found joy in discovering miracles of nature with his sister, and for the high ground that helped them escape the torrent of rain.

Beth She found joy in the close friendship that the family had developed with Mr. Hemstreet, and the provision of someone to teach Sandy.

Myron He found joy in the close friendship that he had developed with the family, the joy of teaching again, and relishing the gifts he was both able to give and receive.

Close out this activity by making it more personal. Ask the students: What are some often overlooked sources of joy in a typical teenager's life?

For the **TOOK ACTIVITY** we will invite the students to **reflect** upon things that have brought them joy in the past year. Ask them to make a list of things that has brought them joy in the past **week**? Have them make a list of the things that has brought them joy in the past **year**?

Challenge them to look for joy in unexpected places in the coming week and then ask:

Would they be willing to share what they found in our next session?

Close the session by thanking God for all the joy that He has brought into their lives in the past year.

> **Memory Verse: Isaiah 61:10** NLT I am overwhelmed with joy in the LORD my God! For he has dressed me with the clothing of salvation and draped me in a robe of righteousness. I am like a bridegroom in his wedding suit or a bride with her jewels.

SESSION PLANNING SHEET

Session Title: __ Kingdom qualities – Joy in His Presence_____ Date: _____

Session Focus: _ God wants us to understand how all the wellsprings of joy can only be found in our relationship with Him.

Session Aims: **KNOW** _ Identify the elements of joy in a believer's life as revealed through various Scriptures. _____

FEEL _ Express the joy that you have experienced through God's presence, and your faith in Him. ____

DO _ Make a list of things that bring joy into your life and review the list each day this coming week.

Session Plan	Session Activities	Preparation
Time:__15min__ **APPROACH**	**Methods, Instructions, Questions** **Bible Project word study Joy** https://www.youtube.com/watch?v=qvOhQTuD2e0 This video gives a brief overview of joy in the Christian life. Instruct the students to write down something new they learned from video. **The British people may be the best in the world at organizing dignified events.** https://www.youtube.com/watch?v=Kav0FEhtLug. **What's right about this? What's wrong about this?**	**Materials** YouTube account Internet access and for larger groups means of projection
Time:__20 min__ **BIBLE EXPLORATION**	**Searching for Joy Fill In the blanks Activity** Fill in the missing words and place the refences in one of the three columns in the table. <table><tr><th colspan="3">Where joy comes from</th></tr><tr><th>Joy is a gift</th><th>Joy is a choice</th><th>Joy in response to God's goodness</th></tr><tr><td>Galatians 5:22-23</td><td>Isaiah 12:2-3</td><td>Nehemiah 12:43</td></tr><tr><td>Romans 15:13</td><td>Philippians 1:4</td><td>Jeremiah 31:12</td></tr><tr><td>Psalms 4:7</td><td>Psalms 28:7</td><td>Luke 1:46-49</td></tr><tr><td>Isaiah 56:7</td><td>Philippians 3:1</td><td>Psalms 16:11</td></tr><tr><td>Acts 13:52</td><td>2 Chronicles 6:41</td><td>Psalms 43:4</td></tr><tr><td>Luke 24:52-53</td><td>Philippians 4:4</td><td>Isaiah 9:3</td></tr><tr><td>Psalms 21:6</td><td>Philippians 2:18</td><td></td></tr></table> **Alternate or Optional Activity - LUKE 15** Ask them to come up with some possible challenges or distractions that kept them from restoring their relationship with God?	NASB, NIV, NLT & NKJV Bibles Pencils Student Personal Study Guides OR Searching for Joy Worksheets
Time:__15 min__ **LIFE IMPLICATIONS**	Using the characters in the short story: "A Closer Walk" give some examples of overlooked sources of joy. Write down what you have found. Remind students of each of these characters from the story: **Sandy** – Special needs daughter, **Blake** – Big brother to Sandy, **Beth** – Sandy & Blake's mom, **Myron** – retired teacher What are some often overlooked sources of joy in a typical teenager's life?	
Time:__10 min__ **APPLICATION**	Make a list of things that has brought them joy in the past **week**. Make a list of things that has brought them joy in the past year. Challenge them to look for joy in unexpected places in the coming week. Would they be willing to share what they found in our next session? Close the session by thanking God for all the joy that He has brought into their lives in the past year.	

Unit Four – Your Kingdom Come – Lesson 17 Joy…Prompts

Has prayer become a duty…a habit…a discipline? God calls us to a place of joyful fellowship in His house of prayer.

Isaiah 56:7 Even those I will bring to My holy mountain And make them joyful in My house of prayer. Their burnt offerings and their sacrifices will be acceptable on My altar; For My house will be called a house of prayer for all the peoples." NASB

It has been said that the one who provides the greatest chance for hope will be given the greatest authority. The world is crying out for hope. Let's point them in the right direction.

Jeremiah 29:7 'Seek the welfare of the city where I have sent you into exile, and pray to the LORD on its behalf; for in its welfare you will have welfare.' NASB

Romans 15:13 Now may the God of hope fill you with all joy and peace in believing, so that you will abound in hope by the power of the Holy Spirit. NASB

If our prayer life helps us see Jesus as He is…the ascended King…worship, praise and joy will be the natural result.

Luke 24:52,53 They worshiped him and then returned to Jerusalem filled with great joy. And they spent all of their time in the Temple, praising God. NLT

The day will come when all our questions will be answered. The answers will be found in our relationship with Jesus. When we really know His heart for us, we will understand both how to ask and what to ask for.

John 16:23,24 And in that day you will ask Me nothing. Most assuredly, I say to you, whatever you ask the Father in My name He will give you. Until now you have asked nothing in My name. Ask, and you will receive, that your joy may be full. NKJV

We speak of God's house as a place of worship, evangelism and teaching/preaching, and so it is. God has called His house a "house of prayer." God makes His people joyful in the house of prayer and their worship is found acceptable.

Isaiah 56:7 these I will bring to my holy mountain and give them joy in my house of prayer. Their burnt offerings and sacrifices will be accepted on my altar; for my house will be called a house of prayer for all nations." NIV

Joy is the unmistakable evidence of being in, or having been in, the presence of God. May this be a day when others know that we have been in Your presence Lord. May our time with You show up in the smile on our face, the skip in our step, and the laughter on our lips.

Psalm 16:11 You will show me the path of life; In Your presence is fullness of joy; At Your right hand are pleasures forevermore. NKJV

Psalm 118:24 This is the day the Lord has made; we will rejoice and be glad in it. NKJV

Who doesn't want their life to be filled with joy and hope and peace? Come….let's nourish our souls by the power of the Holy Spirit. It really is what Christmas is all about!

Romans 15:13 Now may the God of hope fill you with all joy and peace in believing, that you may abound in hope by the power of the Holy Spirit. NKJV

Luke 2:14 "Glory to God in the highest, And on earth peace, goodwill toward men!" NKJV

Lesson Eighteen: Fellowship

Lesson Eighteen is the first of three lessons which will focus on pursuing depth in our connection with God. Unit Five is called Your will be done. It invites us to approach God with devotion. In today's lesson we will focus on how fellowship with God and others is linked to our corporate times of prayer. There is a depth of relationship that grows by truly sharing someone else's burden. That is true with other Christians, and even in sharing the burdens that are on God's heart. God invites us to *"pray to the Lord who is in charge of the harvest; ask him to send more workers into his fields."* NLT God desires that more people enter into a good relationship with Him. When we understand His heart, we will pray for more people to reach out in order to make that happen. This is just one of many ways that we can develop our relationship with God by praying for the things that he deeply cares about. For example: Psalm 34:18 tells us, *"The LORD is close to the brokenhearted; he rescues those whose spirits are crushed."* NLT If we want to get close to God, we will have to get close to them, pray for them, and do what He calls us to do in response. We are going to explore how joining our hearts together in prayer will enhance our relationship with God. We will also look at some of the things that might detract from our connection with God and others.

We will lead off the learning session by illustrating how cooperating with one another can be hard work. The **HOOK ACTIVITY** will ask the students to work as a team to build a pyramid out of plastic cups. Tell them that they cannot touch the cups with their hands or any part of their bodies. They must use rubber bands that have paper clips attached to them. The paper clips are attached to strings of equal lengths. In teams of 4-6 they must pull the rubber band over and around the cup, and then retract it so that they can grasp the cup. Once they maneuver the rubber band and get a hold the cup, they must move it into a desired location. This will be reasonably easy for the bottom layer of the pyramid, but much more challenging for the upper layers. Allow them 2 minutes to practice grasping cups and placing them in a desired position. Then tell them that they will be competing to see which team can build the largest complete pyramid in 5 minutes. Tell them that as a team they have 2 minutes to discuss how large of a pyramid they can build in 5 minutes. They will have to talk about how many cups the team will try to place on each level of the pyramid. A team cannot win without completing the pyramid before the 5 minutes are expired. After the time is up, tell the teams that they have 2 minutes to choose a leader to represent them in sharing with the class what led to their success or failure. What were some of the things that enhanced their efforts, and what detracted from their progress?

If you have a very small group, you can have them all be on the same team. Have them see how fast they can build the pyramid by using their dominant hands. Follow that up with seeing how quickly they can build the pyramid using their least dominant hand. You can talk about how according to 1 Corinthians 12 the Body of Christ needs even the weakest parts. In some ways the weaker parts are more necessary than the parts that we admire most.

Transition to the **BOOK ACTIVITY** by that suggesting God has designed each of us to be in partnership with Him and His people. Our hearts may be instinctively drawn towards selfishness, but that will not lead to real fulfillment. God has placed us in families for a reason. God's people are represented as "the Bride of Christ," "the Family of God," "the Children of God," and "the Body of Christ." All of these illustrate the vital interpersonal element of what it means to be a vibrant Christian. As convenient as it might seem to "go it alone" in our faith walk, God has never really given us that option. As inconvenient as it might be, we actually do need one another in order to flourish. We were designed for interdependence.

With that in mind, we should pay special attention to the kind of things that might enhance or detract from creating that kind of "fellowship." Look up the Scripture verses found in the middle column. In the table below write a word or phrase to describe what will enhance or detract from our fellowship. In most cases you will find answers that will only fit in the Enhance or Detract column. Some of the verses will allow for answers in both columns.

For this activity we can set the learners up in triads (groups of three) to discuss their answers before sharing them with the class.

Enhancing Christian "fellowship" OR NOT		
Key Word/Phrase ENHANCES FELLOWSHIP	Scripture verses	Key Word/Phrase DETRACTS FELLOWSHIP
Proclaiming to others what we have seen and heard about Jesus	1 John 1:3	
Being devoted to four things -biblical teaching, communion- fellowship and prayer	Acts 2:42	
Knowledge of every good thing that is in you	Philemon 1:6	
Walk in the light so that darkness will not overtake you	John 12:35	He who walks in darkness does not know where he is going
	2 Corinthians 6:14	Don't be bound together (in partnership) with unbelievers
Consistent prayer for other believers	Philippians 1:4-5	
	1 John 1:6	When we walk in darkness and do not practice the truth
	Ephesians 5:11	Avoid unfruitful deeds of darkness – even expose them
Participate in the fellowship of His sufferings – attain resurrection	Philippians 3:10-11	
Know (be united as one with) the one true God and His Son Jesus – believe that God sent Him	John 17:3,21	
Be clothed in love	Colossians 3:14	

Become a mature Christian – let Him help you measure up the full standard of being Christ-like	Ephesians 4:13	
Trust in God rather than in our own strengths	1 Corinthians 1:9,10	Trusting in our own strength apart from God leads to spiritual death
Be humble – united in spirit – intent on one purpose	Philippians 2:1-3	
When we walk in the light - the blood of Jesus cleanses us from sin	1 John 1:7	
Warmly welcome (acknowledge) others who are in the faith	Galatians 2:9	
Identify with the fact that there is a part of our lives that has to die and be resurrected to new life	Romans 6:5	
Diligently pursue peace with one another	Ephesians 4:3	
Pray that other Christians will grow (choose any one of the following) in their knowledge of God's will, in their discernment of spiritual things, living in ways that please God, bearing spiritual fruit, and in spiritual power	Philippians 1:7-9	
Pray that other Christians will grow (choose any one of the following) in their love, their knowledge of Christ and their discernment of spiritual things	Colossians 1:9-12	
Follow Christ so you won't walk in darkness	John 8:12	

As an **Alternate BOOK activity** point the class to Acts chapter 12:1-19. In this passage the entire church prays for Peter's release from prison. Give the students 3 x 5" cards with role play assignments. Tell them to have a mock conversation (i.e., role play) representing people assigned to them by the cards they are given. They will have 3-5 minutes to prepare to present their mock conversation to the class.

Role play - person assigned to give the report of Peter's imprisonment to the prayer meeting leader and the way the leader might have responded? What did that conversation possibly look like?

Role Play- Peter sharing his prison escape experience and the response of one of the people who attended the church prayer meeting. What did that conversation possibly look like?

Role Play - Mary the mother of John Mark (several days later) talking with her son (**John Mark**) about the idea of hosting another prayer gathering.

Role play – **Rhoda** talking to **Peter** (a few days later) asking why she responded the way she did at the door and what Peter might have said to her.

Role Play final discussion questions – Throw a ping pong ball or bean bag to someone who was a Role Play character. Have them describe how that character might have felt about united prayer after the Acts 12 prayer meeting. How is that similar to how people feel about prayer meetings in your church today?

Close activity by having the students suggest the kinds of prayers the church might have offered on behalf of Peter.

Whether you used the "Enhance or Detract" table, or the "Acts 12 Role Play" exercise for your Book Activity, you can transition to the **LOOK ACTIVITY** by suggesting that we review the homework short story. What kinds of things helped enhance or detracted from the relationships of the characters? How would praying with others provide a similar role in enhancing or detracting from our connections?

What was the sport that Hank and Gary played that helped them begin to develop a closer relationship? Are any of you on a sports team, play in a band, sing in a chorus, or act in a drama with classmates? How does that help you connect with them? How might praying with others provide a similar connection for people?

How often did Hank and Gary meet at the coffee shop? Do any of you as students have a regular meeting place with other classmates? How does that help you connect with them? How might praying with others provide a similar connection for people?

What prompted Hank to make the commitment to meet with Gary? Has anyone here gotten closer to a classmate when they were hurt in some way? Did that help you connect more closely with them? How might praying with others in those situations provide a similar connection for people?

What provided a distraction to Hank and Gary's close relationship? Does anything like that happen between your classmates? How does that distract you in your connection with them? How might praying with them overcome these kinds of distractions?

What prompted Gahiji to stop and ask Hank to pray with him? Have you ever been asked to pray for someone you don't know? What motivated you to pray for them? How did that time in prayer change your views about that person?

Have you ever been in a prayer meeting with a person of a different race? Have you ever been in a prayer meeting where you were in the racial minority? How did that impact your feelings about that race of people?

Transition to the **HOOK ACTIVITY** by asking the students to list the potential benefits that could come into their lives and in the lives of others through times of prayer. Draw a line down the middle of a White or digital board. Place all answers on one side of the line. Ask them to list where and when their church gathers together for prayer. Write that on the other side of the line. Ask if they would commit themselves to attend that meeting in the coming week. If not, illustrate the loss of benefits by erasing the list of benefits on the board.

Memory Verse: Philippians 1:3,4 I thank my God upon every remembrance of you, always in every prayer of mine making request for you all with joy NKJV

SESSION PLANNING SHEET

Session Title: __Fellowship_____ Date: _____

Session Focus: _To discover some of the things that will enhance or detract from our fellowship when we pray with one another. _

Session Aims: **KNOW** _ Identify the things that can enhance or detract from our fellowship as Christians. _____

FEEL _ Express the satisfaction found in sharing the joys and burdens of other people. _____

DO _ Make a commitment to attend their church's prayer meeting in the coming week._____

Session Plan	Session Activities	Preparation
Time:__15min__ APPROACH	**Methods, Instructions, Questions** Youth Teamwork Activity **Plastic Cup Pyramid Activity** As teams pull on the strings to stretch the rubber bands. Make them large enough to go around the plastic cup …relax the rubber band to grasp the plastic cup. Move the cup into position to create a pyramid. The tallest pyramid built within a 5-minute deadline wins.	**Materials** Plastic cups Rubber bands Paper clips, string
Time:__20 min__ BIBLE EXPLORATION	**Enhancing Christian "fellowship" OR NOT** Review the following Scripture verses and chose how they might enhance or detract from your fellowship with other Christians. 1 John 1:3, Acts 2:42, Philemon 1:6, John 12:35, 2 Corinthians 6:14, Philippians 1:4-5, 1 John 1:6, Ephesians 5:11, Philippians 3:10-11, John 17:3,21, Colossians 3:14, Ephesians 4:13, 1 Corinthians 1:9,10, Philippians 2:1-3, 1 John 1:7, Galatians 2:9, Romans 6:5, Ephesians 4:3, Philippians 1:7-9, Colossians 1:9-12, John 8:12 **Alternate activity:** Acts chapter 12 The entire church prays for Peter's release **Students suggest prayers that the church might have prayed for Peter.** **Acts 12 Characters Role Play- Peter, Report to Mary & her son John Mark, Rhoda Role Play final discussion questions (see teacher's manual)** **Rotating Prayer Role Play –** Bring a ping pong ball or throw bag.	Bibles, pen or pencils, Student Personal Study Guides, OR Enhancing Christian fellowship OR NOT activity worksheet 3x5" Role Play assignment cards Ping Pong ball or bean bag
Time:__15 min__ LIFE IMPLICATIONS	**"DETAILS" multiple choice activity** Use the multiple-choice exercise in the Student Participation Study Guide to illustrate how we might enhance or detract from our relational connections. What are some similar connections you might have with classmates that could lead to opportunities for prayer? **Alternate Activity -** Rotating Prayer Role **Acts 12 Characters Role Play -** Report about imprisonment, Peter, Mary & her son John Mark, Rhoda Role Play final discussion questions (teacher's manual)	Bibles, pen or pencils, Student Personal Study Guides 3x5" Role Play assignment cards Ping Pong ball or bean bag
Time:__10 min__ APPLICATION	**White or Digital board exercise** Draw a vertical line to split the board in half. On the **left half** have the students share the potential benefits that could come to their lives and the lives of others through times of prayer. On the **right half** have the students share when and where their church meets for prayer. Would they commit themselves to attend that meeting this week? Erase the benefits from the left half of the board to show them the benefits that could be lost if they chose not to attend. Close with time of prayer requests and group prayer.	White Board or Digital Board Dry Erase marker and eraser

Unit Four – Your Will Be Done – Lesson 18   Fellowship Prompts

If we want to take our "fellowship" to a whole new level, we must meet with others in heartfelt prayer. If we minimize the importance of praying together, our "koinania" (fellowship) will diminish proportionately.

Philippians 1:3,4   I thank my God upon every remembrance of you, always in every prayer of mine making request for you all with joy.   NKJV

Philemon 1:6   and I pray that the fellowship of your faith may become effective through the knowledge of every good thing which is in you for Christ's sake.   NASB

There are workers who are "in tight" with the Boss, who know the blueprints, the plan, the ultimate results needed for the project, and others who just take orders. The difference affects every element of their work.

John 15:15   I no longer call you servants, because a servant does not know his master's business. Instead, I have called you friends, for everything that I learned from my Father I have made known to you.   NIV

From the very beginning there have been four vital facets of Christianity: the careful teaching of God's truth, hearts joined in genuine fellowship, celebration of communion, and coming before God in prayer. In every generation God's people are continually devoted to all four.

Acts 2:42   They were continually devoting themselves to the apostles' teaching and to fellowship, to the breaking of bread, and to prayer.   NASB

God's purpose for mankind has always been for us to live in fellowship with Him. Our prayer life is a reflection of fulfilling God's plan for our lives.

Jeremiah 31:3   The LORD appeared to him from afar, saying, "I have loved you with an everlasting love; Therefore, I have drawn you with lovingkindness.   NASB

Why make prayer more difficult than it really is? We were created to be in fellowship with God. How hard is it for an infant to listen for their mother's voice, or for a mother to hear a baby's cry?

Isaiah 49:14-15   But Zion said, "The Lord has forsaken me, And my Lord has forgotten me." "Can a woman forget her nursing child, And not have compassion on the son of her womb? Surely they may forget, Yet I will not forget you.   NKJV

What makes a friend really special? The list might include: long relaxed conversations, shared secrets, common interests, a desire to participate in the things they care about. I guess you could say that you love being with them and they love being with you.

John 15:9-12   "I have loved you even as the Father has loved me. Remain in my love. When you obey me, you remain in my love, just as I obey my Father and remain in his love. I have told you this so that you will be filled with my joy. Yes, your joy will overflow! I command you to love each other in the same way that I love you.   NLT

Believers are only righteous before God through Christ's work on the cross, yet God asks us to be open about the fact that we sometimes fail to live in a righteous way. Our prayers are most effective when we are living in fellowship with God and His family.

Psalm 34:15   The eyes of the Lord are on the righteous, And His ears are open to their cry.   NKJV

Lesson Nineteen: Submission

Lesson Nineteen is the second of three lessons which will focus on pursuing depth in our connection with God. Unit Five is called Your will be done. It invites us to approach God with devotion. In today's lesson we will focus on what it might mean to see God's will being done on earth as it is in heaven. In order to gain some insight into this we will take a closer look at what heaven might look like. We will examine what will, and will not be found in heaven. Let's start with the premise that God will have complete sovereignty in heaven. There won't be any room for rebellion, resistance or defiance. A perfect example of this would be Satan's attempt at rebellion, and the fact that he was expelled from heaven. While he still has some limited access, he ultimately will be permanently banished.

The Scriptures reference traits of those who will, and will not be found in heaven. They also tell us how His will can, and will be done there. For the sake of brevity, we will limit the scope of our search to three categories. We will review Scriptures which reflect on who Jesus said would be, or would not be found in heaven. We will also review Scriptures which reflect on who the Apostles, Luke and the author of Hebrews said would be, or would not be found in heaven. We then will review the Scriptures which reflect on what and who the Apostle John said would be, or would not be found in heaven. These three categories will also include the characteristics of those who will be found there.

The **HOOK ACTIVITY** helps us raise the question that would likely precede our discussion of what heaven will look like. Before we focus on what heaven will be like, we might want to address the question of the student's belief about the afterlife. A good way to lead into this topic is to invite the students to view the following Prager University video. It is entitled: **Is There An Afterlife? By Denis Prager.** https://www.prageru.com/video/is-there-life-after-this-life/ Mr. Prager is a well-known philosopher and commentator. His religious background is Jewish, but his commentary is very well accepted in the Christian community. This clip answers the question of "Is there an afterlife?" by postulating that if there is a "just God" there has to be an afterlife. What is that afterlife going to be like? Dennis Prager says he doesn't know. If we accept the premise that the existence of a "just God" demands an afterlife, we can legitimately presume that such a God would want us to know what that afterlife would be like. This helps us make the transition to the **BOOK ACTIVITY**, where we will look at three different sources of such a revelation of the afterlife: the words of Jesus, several Apostles, and especially the Apostle John.

Invite the students to use their Student Personal Study Guides to prepare and/or share their answers to the things/traits of those who are found in heaven. There are three tables that list the Scriptures that will help them find those people, traits, or things, that will be, or will not be found in heaven. If they don't have the Student Personal Study Guides, then use the FOUND OR NOT FOUND IN HEAVEN worksheets that can be found in the Teacher's resource packet/CD.

	This will be in heaven Traits of those in heaven	This will not be in heaven Traits of those not in heaven
According to Jesus		
Matthew 5:12	Reward	
Matthew 7:13-14	Few who find life	Many who find destruction
Matthew 8:11-12	Abraham, Isaac & Jacob	sons of the kingdom (Israel)
John 14:2-3	A place Jesus prepared for us	
Matthew 10:32-33	Those who confess Jesus	Those who do not confess Jesus
Luke 23:42-43	The repentant thief on cross	
Matthew 13:40-43	Righteous ones	Stumbling blocks & lawless
Matthew 18:3-4	Those who humble themselves	
Matthew 18:10	Angels of little children	
Matthew 22:29-32	Angels, Abraham, Isaac & Jacob	
Matthew 23:29,33		Scribes & Pharisees
Luke 13:24,27-29	Abraham, Isaac & Jacob and prophets of the kingdom	Evildoers
Matthew 25:30		Worthless slaves
John 5:24-29	Those who hear Jesus' words and believe in Him	
Matthew 25:41-46		Accursed ones, devil and his angels

FOUND OR NOT FOUND IN HEAVEN EXERCISE

	This will be in heaven Traits of those in heaven	This will not be in heaven Traits of those not in heaven
According to the Apostles, Luke & whoever wrote Hebrews		
Acts 17:30-31	Those who repent	Those who do not repent
Romans 1:18-20		No ungodliness, nor those who suppress the truth in unrighteousness
Romans 2:4-10	Those who persevere in doing good	Stubborn unrepentant hearts, nor the selfishly ambitious who do not obey the truth
1 Corinthians 6:9-11	Such were some of you, but you were sanctified	Unrighteous, Fornicators, Idolaters, Adulterers, Effeminate, Homosexuals, Thieves, Covetous, Drunkards, Revilers, Swindlers Unrepentant
Galatians 5:19-21		Those who practice the deeds of the flesh
Ephesians 1:18-22	Inheritance of the saints Jesus Christ ruling over all	
Ephesians 2:3-7	Saints seated with Christ	
Ephesians 5:5-7		No immoral or impure or covetous person, no idolaters, sons of disobedience
Philippians 3:19-21	Those who eagerly wait for a Savior, the Lord Jesus Christ	Those who minds are set on earthly things
Colossians 3:1-6	Christ seated at the right hand of God	Impure people, sons of darkness
2 Thessalonians 1:6-9		Those who afflict Christians
Hebrews 1:2-3,8:1,12:2	God's son sitting at the right hand of the Majesty on high	
1 Peter 1:3-5	An inheritance which is imperishable and undefiled	
2 Peter 2:4,9	Godly	No rebellious angels, no unrighteous
2 Peter 3:13	Righteousness	

	This will be in heaven Traits of those in heaven	This will not be in heaven Traits of those not in heaven
According to the Apostle John		
John 3:15-18	Those who believe in Jesus	Those who do not believe
John 3:36	Those who believe in the Son	Those who do not obey the Son
1 John 2:16-17	The one who does the will of God lives forever	
Revelation 7:11	angels, elders, four living creatures	
Revelation 7:13-14	Elders, Those who came through the tribulation	
Revelation 7:16	water of life	Hunger, thirst, sun beating down on them, heat
Revelation 7:17	Lamb on the throne guide them to the springs of the water of life	tears
Revelation 20:10-14	Great White Throne, book of life	Devil, Beast, death, Hades
Revelation 20:15		Anyone without their name written in the book of life
Revelation 21:4		tears, death, sorrow, crying, pain
Revelation 21:8		cowardly, unbelieving, abominable, murderers, sorcerers, sexually immoral, idolaters, liars
Revelation 21:22-27	Those whose names are written in the book of Life	No temple, no sun, no moon, no night, no gates, nothing unclean, no one who practices abominations and lying
Revelation 22:2	Tree of life The leaves will be for the healing of the nations	
Revelation 22:3	Servants of God reigning	No longer any curse
Revelation 22:5	Saints who will reign	No longer any night

You can wrap up the BOOK ACTIVITY using Popcorn responses about what will be found in heaven. Write their responses on a white or digital board. Then, on a second board, have them give Popcorn responses to what will not be found in heaven. Write a brief summary of what doing God's will might look like there.

Now, let's explore what God has revealed about what it looks like to do His will here on earth. There are many elements to finding and fulfilling God's will here on earth. One of them would be learning what it means to submit to those to whom God has given authority.

Before we look at what the Bible says about that, you might want to give a brief caveat about the fact that God would not want the students to submit in abusive situations. Tell the students that we will discuss this in even greater detail in a later lesson. For now, simply tell them that there are people they can look to for help if they think that abuse may be involved. Suggest that teachers, pastors, or the police could be someone they could turn to in an abusive situation.

Having excluded "abusive situations," we will now look at the agencies or people to whom God has given authority in our lives. We will do this by having them work on the His Will On Earth Exercise from their Student Personal Study Guides. In this exercise review the Scripture verses, and circle the God ordained person or agency referenced in that passage. A case could be made for multiple choices for each passage. Select the one that is the best fit. All of the verses are from the New King James Bible.

Romans 13:1-2 Let every soul be subject to the governing authorities. For there is no authority except from God, and the authorities that exist are appointed by God. Therefore, whoever resists the authority resists the ordinance of God, and those who resist will bring judgment on themselves.

JESUS   GOVERNMENT   PASTOR/ELDER   ONE ANOTHER   PARENTS   SPOUSE

Ephesians 1:20-22 which He worked in Christ when He raised Him from the dead and seated *Him* at His right hand in the heavenly *places,* far above all principality and power and might and dominion, and every name that is named, not only in this age but also in that which is to come. And He put all *things* under His feet, and gave Him *to be* head over all *things* to the church.

JESUS   GOVERNMENT   PASTOR/ELDER   ONE ANOTHER   PARENTS   SPOUSE

Colossians 3:20 Children, obey your parents in all things, for this is well pleasing to the Lord.

JESUS   GOVERNMENT   PASTOR/ELDER   ONE ANOTHER   PARENTS   SPOUSE

Hebrews 13:17 Obey those who rule over you, and be submissive, for they watch out for your souls, as those who must give account. Let them do so with joy and not with grief, for that would be unprofitable for you.

JESUS   GOVERNMENT   PASTOR/ELDER   ONE ANOTHER   PARENTS   SPOUSE

Titus 2:9 Exhort bondservants to be obedient to their own masters, to be well pleasing in all *things,* not answering back.

JESUS   GOVERNMENT   PASTOR/ELDER   ONE ANOTHER   PARENTS   SPOUSE

Philippians 2:10-11 that at the name of Jesus every knee should bow, of those in heaven, and of those on earth, and of those under the earth, and *that* every tongue should confess that Jesus Christ *is* Lord, to the glory of God the Father.

JESUS   GOVERNMENT   PASTOR/ELDER   ONE ANOTHER   PARENTS   SPOUSE

Ephesians 5:22 Wives, submit yourselves to your own husbands as you do to the Lord.

JESUS   GOVERNMENT   PASTOR/ELDER   ONE ANOTHER   PARENTS   SPOUSE

John 17:2 as You have given Him authority over all flesh, that He should give eternal life to as many as You have given Him. as You have given Him authority over all flesh, that He [a]should give eternal life to as many as You have given Him.

JESUS   GOVERNMENT   PASTOR/ELDER   ONE ANOTHER   PARENTS   SPOUSE

1 Peter 5:5 Likewise you younger people, submit yourselves to your elders. Yes, all of *you* be submissive to one another, and be clothed with humility, for "God resists the proud,
But gives grace to the humble."

JESUS   GOVERNMENT   PASTOR/ELDER   ONE ANOTHER   PARENTS   SPOUSE

Colossians 4:1 Masters, give your bondservants what is just and fair, knowing that you also have a Master in heaven.

JESUS   GOVERNMENT   PASTOR/ELDER   ONE ANOTHER   PARENTS   SPOUSE

1 Corinthians 16:15-16 I urge you, brethren—you know the household of Stephanas, that it is the first fruits of Achaia, and *that* they have devoted themselves to the ministry of the saints— [16] that you also submit to such, and to everyone who works and labors with *us.* I urge you, brethren—you know the household of Stephanas, that it is the first fruits of Achaia, and *that* they have devoted themselves to the ministry of the saints—that you also submit to such, and to everyone who works and labors with *us.*

JESUS   GOVERNMENT   PASTOR/ELDER   ONE ANOTHER   PARENTS   SPOUSE

Ephesians 6:1 Children, obey your parents in the Lord, for this is right.

JESUS   GOVERNMENT   PASTOR/ELDER   ONE ANOTHER   PARENTS   SPOUSE

Matthew 28:18 And Jesus came and spoke to them, saying, "All authority has been given to Me in heaven and on earth.

JESUS   GOVERNMENT   PASTOR/ELDER   ONE ANOTHER   PARENTS   SPOUSE

1 Thessalonians 5:12-13 And we urge you, brethren, to recognize those who labor among you, and are over you in the Lord and [a]admonish you, and to esteem them very highly in love for their work's sake. Be at peace among yourselves.

JESUS   GOVERNMENT   PASTOR/ELDER   ONE ANOTHER   PARENTS   SPOUSE

Colossians 3:22-23 Bondservants, obey in all things your masters according to the flesh, not with eyeservice, as men-pleasers, but in sincerity of heart, fearing God. And whatever you do, do it heartily, as to the Lord and not to men.

JESUS   GOVERNMENT   PASTOR/ELDER   ONE ANOTHER   PARENTS   SPOUSE

Titus 3:1 Remind them to be subject to rulers and authorities, to obey, to be ready for every good work.

JESUS   GOVERNMENT   PASTOR/ELDER   ONE ANOTHER   PARENTS   SPOUSE

Colossians 3:24 knowing that from the Lord you will receive the reward of the inheritance; for you serve the Lord Christ.

JESUS   GOVERNMENT   PASTOR/ELDER   ONE ANOTHER   PARENTS   SPOUSE

Philippians 2:12 Therefore, my beloved, as you have always obeyed, not as in my presence *only, but now much more in my absence, work out your own salvation with fear and* trembling.

JESUS   GOVERNMENT   PASTOR/ELDER   ONE ANOTHER   PARENTS   SPOUSE

Ephesians 5:21

submitting to one another in the fear of God.

JESUS   GOVERNMENT   PASTOR/ELDER   ONE ANOTHER   PARENTS   SPOUSE

Colossians 1:16-17 For by Him all things were created that are in heaven and that are on earth, visible and invisible, whether thrones or dominions or principalities or powers. All things were created through Him and for Him. And He is before all things, and in Him all things consist.

JESUS   GOVERNMENT   PASTOR/ELDER   ONE ANOTHER   PARENTS   SPOUSE

You can summarize the key agencies that God has placed in authority for each of us. At some point they will likely be in one of these positions of responsibility. As a teenager, they are probably not there yet, but eventually they will likely assume more than one of these roles. When they do, they will see the great value of God's purpose in wanting us to understand submission. If time permits, you may want to review the motivations that we might find for submitting. I would suggest that there are at least 4 motivations that might help us understand and accept the idea of submitting to one another.

1) **I submit because God has instructed me to do so.**   How might this be the right motivation? How might this be a wrong motivation?
2) **I submit because I am forced to submit.** How might this be the right motivation? How might this be a wrong motivation?
3) **I submit because consequences of disobedience are severe.** How might this be the right motivation? How might this be a wrong motivation?
4) **I submit because I want to...because this is the best thing for me.** How might this be the right motivation?

You can transition to the **TOOK ACTIVITY** by suggesting that it is important that we find the right motivation for doing God's will on earth. Most of us will find that challenging at times. We should recognize that God is more than willing to help us with that. How we think on this issue will help us a lot. Make a list of reasons why submitting to each of the God ordained authorities might be a good thing for you.

Jesus   Government   Pastors/elders   One another   Parents   Spouse

(Personal reflection) Which of these do you find most challenging?

Will you commit yourself to pray every day this week for God to help you submit to the most challenging authorities/agencies/people on that list?

TEACHER'S NOTE: You might want to look over the next Session Planning Sheet. If you choose the first element of the HOOK ACTIVITY, you will want to pull up some plants and let them die/become dry before the next lesson.

Memory Verse: Matthew 28:19-20 NIV "Go and make disciples of all nations, baptizing them in the name of the Father and of the Son and of the Holy Spirit, and teaching them to obey everything I have commanded you. And surely I am with you always, to the very end of the age."

SESSION PLANNING SHEET

Session Title: __ Submission – Your will be done on earth as it is in heaven _____ Date: _____

Session Focus: _ In Jesus model for prayer, He encourages us to pray that God's will be done on earth as it is in heaven. ___

Session Aims: **KNOW** _ Identify the traits of those who will be in heaven and how His will can and will be done there.__

FEEL _ Express a desire for God's help in learning why submission to His will is the best thing for you. _

DO _ Make a commitment to pray for God's help with your most challenging submission concern. __

Session Plan	Session Activities	Preparation
Time:__15min__ **APPROACH**	**Methods, Instructions, Questions** **Dennis Prager Is There An Afterlife?** https://www.prageru.com/video/is-there-life-after-this-life/This clip answers the question: "Is there an afterlife?" It postulates that if there is a just God there must be an afterlife. What is that afterlife going to be like? Dennis Prager says he doesn't know. If there is a God, He would want us to know what a "just afterlife" would look like. We will look at three different sources of such a revelation of the afterlife. The words of Jesus, several Apostles, and the Apostle John.	**Materials** Access to a You Tube account, means of projection
Time:__20 min__ **BIBLE EXPLORATION**	Let's start by taking a look at what will be found and not found in heaven. That might help us understand what "Your will be done on earth as it is in heaven" might really mean. **Found or Not Found in Heaven exercise** According to Jesus, what will and will not be found in heaven? According to the Apostles, Luke and the author of Hebrews, what will and will not be found in heaven? According to the Apostle John, what will and will not be found in heaven?	Bibles, Pens or Pencils, **Found or NOT Found in Heaven Exercise** in Student Participation Study Guide or worksheets
Time:__15 min___ **LIFE IMPLICATIONS**	**His Will On Earth Exercise** ***(Caveat about abusive situations)*** After each verse circle the agency or person to whom we are instructed to submit. JESUS GOVERNMENT PASTOR/ELDER ONE ANOTHER PARENTS SPOUSE **MOTIVATIONS** I submit because God has instructed me to do so. Right/wrong? I submit because I am forced to submit. Right/wrong? I submit because consequences of disobedience are severe. Right/Wrong? I submit because I want to...this is the best thing for me. Right/Wrong?	Bibles, Pens or Pencils, Student Participation Study Guides or His Will On Earth worksheets
Time:__10 min__ **APPLICATION**	Make a list of reasons why submitting to each of the God ordained authorities might be a good thing for you. **Jesus Government Pastors/elders One another Parents Spouse** (Personal reflection) Which of these do you find most challenging? Will you commit yourself to pray every day this week for God to help you submit to the most challenging authorities/agencies/people on that list? **ONE OF THE BEST WAYS TO HELP IS TO PRAY FOR THOSE IN NEED...** Group Prayer: Take personal prayer requests and have students pray for each other.	3 x 5" cards Pens/Pencils

Session Planning Sheet ©2013 Dale Roy Erickson, adapted from material found in *Creative Bible Teaching* © 1998 by Lawrence O. Richards and Gary J. Bredfeldt, Moody Publishers. Used by permission.

Unit Five – Your Will Be Done – Lesson 19   Submission Prompts

Submission may be one of the most significant aspects of prayer. No one can be effective in their prayer life without it. It is also one of the most powerful weapons in our warfare (resistance) against our enemy. Our enemy will use a lot of his resources to distract our attention from this vital facet of our spiritual life. Why? That weapon will send him running for cover.

James 4:7 Submit therefore to God. Resist the devil and he will flee from you NKJV

Pity is a natural response to seeing the images of starving children. That is a "godlike" feeling. Some may manipulate the desperation of others with less than pure intentions, but we cannot let that quiet the voice of God. Ask Him. He'll tell you what you can and must do.

2 Samuel 22:7 "In my distress I called upon the LORD, Yes, I cried to my God; And from His temple He heard my voice, And my cry for help came into His ears. NASB

If we really want to walk with God today, we might want to start by asking where He's going.

Amos 3:3 Can two people walk together without agreeing on the direction? NLT
Isaiah 30:21 Your ears shall hear a word behind you, saying, "This is the way, walk in it," Whenever you turn to the right hand or whenever you turn to the left. NKJV

God's Word shows us that there are many ways to come before God in worship. You can stand with your hands lifted high, fall to your knees, or lay down on the ground. But none is of any effect without a heart of submission.

James 4:7 Submit yourselves, then, to God. Resist the devil, and he will flee from you NIV

Who hasn't either said or heard the following? "I said: 'That is enough! We aren't going to talk about this anymore!'" We are God's children and sometimes that is His answer.

Deuteronomy 3:25,26 Let me go over and see the good land beyond the Jordan--that fine hill country and Lebanon." But because of you the LORD was angry with me and would not listen to me. "That is enough," the LORD said. "Do not speak to me anymore about this matter. NIV

Do we see ourselves in prayer as the (CEO) Chief Operating Officers of our lives, or coming to receive our directives from the CEO of the universe?

John 5:30 But I do nothing without consulting the Father. I judge as I am told. And my judgment is absolutely just, because it is according to the will of God who sent me; it is not merely my own. NLT

If you are in a foreign land where most of the people don't speak your language, you will probably need a guide. It would help if that person knows what you need, and how to get you where you need to go. It would probably also help if you stopped talking long enough to listen to them.

Hebrews 11:16 But as it is, they desire a better country, that is, a heavenly one. Therefore God is not ashamed to be called their God; for He has prepared a city for them. NASB
Isaiah 30:21 Whether you turn to the right or to the left, your ears will hear a voice behind you, saying, "This is the way; walk in it." NASB

Lesson Twenty: Abiding

Lesson Twenty is the third of three lessons which will focus on pursuing depth in our connection with God. Unit Five is called Your will be done. It invites us to approach God with devotion. In today's lesson we will again focus on what it means to see God's will being done on earth. The critical truth emphasized in this lesson would be understanding that "God's will being done on earth as it is in heaven" is impossible through human effort alone. We will take a long path to help the students embrace this truth. We will highlight many of the elements of God's will as outlined in the Scriptures. No doubt along the way each student will be able to identify an area where they find that doing God's will is difficult, or impossible. Why would Jesus instruct us to pray that "God's will be done on earth as it is in heaven" if it cannot be done? The truth is that it can be done, but there is only one way that can happen. We will need God's power operative in our lives. Whether we call that "abiding in Christ" or "walking in the Spirit" or "living the transformed life," the core truth is that only God can make it possible and we get to participate in the transformation process. The description of how this happens will differ depending on your denominational tenets, but everyone agrees that it will require God's power.

For the purposes of this lesson we will utilize the phrase "abiding in Christ" when referring to our need for God's power and our active role in gaining access to it. The most poignant Scriptures addressing this element are the memory verses for this lesson. These verses are **John 15:7-9** NIV *If you remain in me and my words remain in you, ask whatever you wish, and it will be given you. This is to my Father's glory, that you bear much fruit, showing yourselves to be my disciples. "As the Father has loved me, so have I loved you. Now remain in my love.* According to these verses our directive is to remain (i.e., remain in Me and let My words remain in you, and remain in My love. If we choose to "remain" in those things, we can ask whatever we wish, we will bring glory to the Father, we will bear much fruit, and we will show ourselves to be His disciples. Jesus used the illustration of being branches that stay attached to the vine. This would be an illustration that nearly all of His disciples would have easily understood. Your students may have far less personal experience with horticulture, so we may need to help them with this illustration.

There are basically two pedagogical tracks for this lesson. Choose whichever one works best for you. It is not likely that you will have enough time to take both paths. One approach will be more focused on the specifics of what the Scriptures tell us about God's will on earth. The second would feature the vine and branches illustration that Jesus used in John chapter 15. Either track will lead the students to the conclusion that the source for an abundant, God honoring life is supernatural. You will see the first path featured in the session outline, and the second one will be listed as alternative activities.

The **HOOK ACTIVITY** for this lesson challenges the students to reveal their natural place or standing in their class at school. We all know that there is a pecking order amongst their peers. We will begin with a 3-minute group discussion as to what measures are used in their school to garner respect or status. After the initial discussion, continue this activity by having the students stand in a single line facing straight towards you. Have them place their hands straight out and place them on the shoulders of the person in front of them. This will set the spacing needed to start this exercise.

This is kind of a spin-off of musical chairs. Suggest that we are looking to establish how much respect they deserve. Have them move forward or back in the line based on the measures of status that they possess. They will need to convince those in front or in back of them that they deserve a different position. They can feel free to suggest that others need to move forward or backward in the line. Make it clear that there can be no pushing or shoving in this exercise.

Start the music. Tell them that when the music stops, they have to remain in that position. While the music is playing, they can attempt to convince people that they need to move forward, or that others need to move back in the line. When you stop the music, you can ask them to reflect on how they feel about their place in the line. **After a short time of reflection, tell them to turn the line around to face in the opposite direction.** Tell them that Jesus is at the front of the line that serves people. Mark 10:45 tells us *"He came not to be served, but to serve and to give His life a ransom for many."* If we want to emulate His life, one of the measures will be surrendering our place in line for the sake of others. **Matthew 19:30** could be brought in at this point: *"Then He said, "But many who are first will be last, and many who are last will be first."* Some people call that "dying to ourselves". We will learn more about that in today's lesson.

ALTERNATE HOOK ACTIVITY

If you select the John 15 vine and branches pedagogical track, you can start the lesson by showing the class, a dead lifeless plant. You should have cut this plant out of the soil at the end of the last lesson. Ask the students what this plant is lacking…i.e., why is it dry and lifeless? What would it take to bring it back to life? Some of the answers should be that it has been cut off from water, nutrients, sunshine, etc. Plants need these vital elements in order to flourish. What would be some of the vital elements that we need in our lives so that we can flourish? We need the power of God (His life within us), we need nutrients (the Word of God) feeding our souls, and fellowship with other believers (life sustaining roots). One critical component of staying attached to these key elements of this would be time spent in prayer…connecting with God.

Whichever track you choose for this lesson you can transition to the **BOOK ACTIVITY** by saying that it is a natural thing for a person to pursue a "selfish motivation" in life. Jesus calls us to flip that upside down and through His strength and power pursue a "God centered and others centered" motivation. That's not the way we are naturally wired. That kind of life requires a true transformation. God's power and His love (i.e. His Spirit in us) can make this possible. His love produces a supernatural flow of power in our lives. It looks like this…Jesus creates a wellspring of love flowing into and out of our lives. The supernatural response is expressed in obedience to God flowing through our lives.

We talked about following God's will in our lives a little bit last week. We have to understand that it isn't a matter of trying harder to obey God through determined effort. It is a matter of the wellspring of Jesus' love being expressed in obedience through us. Once we embrace this new paradigm, we will find that pursuing God's will is not an obligation…it is a supernatural cause and effect of abiding in Christ. The natural and supernatural effect of a rose bud would be the beautiful aroma produced by the rose plant. The observation of those who stop to smell the roses would be the pleasing aroma and beauty of a rose in full bloom. All the rose blossom had to do to create this effect would be to stay connected to the branch. In like manner, when we stay connected to the love of Christ, the natural outflow would be obedience to the will of God which creates the aroma of Christ. 2 Corinthians 2:14-16 $_{TLB}$ says it this way: But thanks be to God! For through what Christ has done, he has triumphed over us so that now wherever we go he uses us to tell others about the Lord and to spread the Gospel like a sweet perfume. As far as God is concerned there is a sweet, wholesome fragrance in our lives. It is the fragrance of Christ within us, an aroma to both the saved and the unsaved all around us. To those who are not being saved, we seem to be a fearful smell of death and doom, while to those who know Christ, we are a life-giving aroma.

It's God's work…not our work. It's God's life in us. Let's take a look at how pursuing God's will by staying connected to the branch is as simple as A.B.C. Divide up into groups of three and discuss what that might mean by reviewing some of the elements of "Your will be done on earth, as it is in heaven."

Review the Scriptures listed in the right columns, and in the left tab/column rank the clarity of God's will using the following measures. Rank them using numbers 1-3.

1. This is a **clear and direct expression** of God's will for every human being.
2. This calls for a **specific plan, behavior or activity** that God wants in each of our lives.
3. This represents **a principle** that all Christians should live by in their daily lives.

In this teacher's manual the verses are summarized for the sake of brevity. You can look them up to get the exact wording and/or full context. This activity will produce a variety of answers. More than one response could be correct depending on the way they shape their answer. Here in the teacher's manual, I will give my selection without reflecting on all the nuances that I would give to the answers. Ranking of a Scripture between 2 or 3 will often be a "teacher's choice."

GOD'S WILL IS AS SIMPLE AS A.B.C.	
A. 1	A. Exodus 20:2-3 I am the Lord your God. You shall have no other Gods before Me.
B. 1	B. 2 Peter 3:9 It is not God's will that any should perish, but that all should come to repentance.
C. 1	C. 1 Thessalonians 4:3 It is God's will that you be sanctified and abstain from sexual immorality.

D. 1	D. Luke 10:27 Love the Lord your God with all your heart and with all your soul and with all your strength and with all your mind; and love your neighbor as yourself.
E. 1	E. Exodus 20:13 You shall not murder.
F. 1	F. John 6:40 God desires that everyone sees the Son and believes in Him.
G. 2,3	G. 1 Thessalonians 5:18 In everything give thanks.
H. 2,3	H. Proverbs 3:5 Trust in the Lord with all your heart and don't lean on your own understanding.
I. 1	I. Exodus 20:7 Don't take the name of the Lord in vain.
J. 1	J. Matthew 28:19 Go into all the world and preach the gospel.
K. 2,3	K. Romans 12:2 Be transformed by the renewing of your mind so that you may prove that the will of God is good and acceptable and perfect.
L. 1	L. Acts 2:38 Repent and be baptized for the forgiveness of your sins and you will receive the gift of the Holy Spirit.
M 1	M. 1 Peter 2:15 It is God's will that by doing good you should silence foolish people.
N. 1	N. Exodus 20:12 Honor your father and mother.
O. 2	O. Luke 9:23 Whoever wants to be my disciple must deny himself, take up his cross and follow me.
P. 1	P. Matthew 22:39 You shall love your neighbor as yourself.
Q. 2	Q. 1 Thessalonians 5:17 Pray without ceasing.
R. 1	R. 1 Timothy 2:3-4 God desires that all people be saved and come to the knowledge of the truth.

S. 1	S. Exodus 20:14 Don't commit adultery.
T. 2,3	T. Ephesians 5:18 Do not get drunk with wine, but be filled with the Holy Spirit.
U. 2,3	U. Micah 6:8 And what does the Lord require of you? To act justly and to love mercy and to walk humbly with your God.
V. 1	V. Ephesians 6:1,2 Children, obey your parents in the Lord, for this is right.
W. 1	W. Exodus 20:15 You shall not steal.
X. 1	X. 1 Peter 1:15,16 You shall be holy (in your behavior), for I am holy.
Y. 1	Y. Matthew 5:48 You shall be perfect, as your Father in Heaven is perfect.
Z. 1	Z. John 13:34 You shall love one another as I have loved you.

ALTERNATE BOOK ACTIVITY

If you chose the lifeless branch track, you might want to use the following exercise for the alternate BOOK ACTIVITY. Introduce this activity by suggesting that there are 5 "Rs" to understanding what it means to Remain in the Lord. Before we look at those elements, we need to understand that we not only need to be connected to the vine, but that the kind of vine we are connected to determines our fruit.

We will use a blindfolded taste test to illustrate this truth. Look for volunteers who are willing to be blindfolded and taste test some foods in an attempt to identify them. SUGGEST THAT VOLUNTEERS MUST NOT HAVE ALLERGIES TO FRUITS OR BERRIES. The volunteers will not be able to use their sense of sight, but can use touch, smell and taste in that order. Some of the potential items could include: **Apple, Pear, Banana, Orange, Plum, Blueberry, Avocado, Peach, Strawberry, or Raisin.** Ask them how they were able to identify each item without actually seeing them. Ask them what these items had to achieve in order to become that kind of fruit or berry. The answer is that they simply had to remain attached to the root and branch system. The kind of plant they were attached to determines the result.

That will be true in each of our lives as well. Others through observation can come to know the kind of root/branch system to which we have been attached. If the root/branch system produces sweetness they will know. If the root/branch system produces bitterness they will see that as well. If we want them to see love, joy, peace, forbearance, kindness, goodness, faithfulness, gentleness, and self-control, we will have to be connected to the Holy Spirit.

How do we do that? That's where the 5 "Rs" of remaining in the Lord might be helpful. 1. **R**emember it's His work Ephesians 2:10,   2. **R**est in the Lord Isaiah 26:3-4, 3. **R**elax…God's in control Isaiah 41:10, 4. **R**evitalize by drawing upon the Spirit's power Romans 8:11 and 5. Leave the **R**esults with God Luke 12:31-32.

You can now transition to the **LOOK ACTIVITY** by calling the students attention back to today's memory verse. We have already highlighted the fact that when we remain in Him, God will bring 4 things into our lives: 1. We will have free access to God in prayer. 2. What we do will bring glory to the Father. 3. We will bear much fruit. 4. We will reveal that we are His disciples. None of these outcomes are likely to come our way if we don't remain in Him…i.e., if God's power is not operative in our lives. If His will and power are central to our motivations, there is no reason for God to withhold these four outcomes. It is, in fact, God's purpose for our lives. A good way to remember this truth would be found in memorizing the first question of the Westminster Catechism. Centuries ago this catechism was used to train people in the essentials of the faith. The very first question is: What is the chief end of man? The answer is: To glorify God and enjoy Him forever. Their training involved memorizing this and other questions and answers. Today we are going to help everyone in this group memorize this within 3 minutes.

Write the words on a white board or digital board. Have the entire class recite the question and the answer twice. Erase one word and ask for a volunteer to repeat the question and answer correctly in spite of the missing word. Then have the entire class repeat the question and answer with the one missing word. When you are done with that select another word to erase and repeat the volunteer/group recitation process. Continue this process until all the words have been removed from the board. Within 3 minutes the entire group should be able to give the entire question and answer word perfect without any of the words appearing on the board. At the very end of the class, ask for a volunteer to repeat the question and answer for you one more time.

ALTERNATE LOOK ACTIVITY:

If you have chosen the lifeless branch track, you could transition to this alternate LOOK ACTIVITY. We have already seen what a lifeless branch looks like and discussed what might be required for a branch to be truly filled with life. We have already said that some of the key elements for a Christian who would be filled with life would be the following: We need the power of God (His life within us), we need nutrients (the Word of God) feeding our souls, and fellowship with other believers (life sustaining roots). What would that really look like? St. Francis of Assisi recorded a prayer of what he thought that might look like. TEACHER'S NOTE: Some scholars suggest that while this prayer is attributed to St. Francis of Assisi, it is unlikely that he was the actual author. This prayer is very SELF focused…make me an instrument…let me…let me not...etc. They suggest that this kind of focus was inconsistent with his life and other writings. Nonetheless, it has become known as The Prayer of St. Francis of Assisi. This is probably not worth bringing up with the class, but this is more of a teacher's awareness note.

It reads as follows:

Lord, make me an instrument of your peace.
Where there is hatred, let me bring love. Where there is offense, let me bring pardon.
Where there is discord, let me bring union. Where there is error, let me bring truth.
Where there is doubt, let me bring faith. Where there is despair, let me bring hope.
Where there is darkness, let me bring your light. Where there is sadness, let me bring joy.
O Master, let me not seek as much to be consoled as to console,
to be understood as to understand, to be loved as to love, for it is in giving that one receives,
it is in self-forgetting that one finds, it is in pardoning that one is pardoned,
it is in dying that one is raised to eternal life.

Let's break this down into individual pieces. Think of FB or Twitter posts that people share. Can you give me an example of someone you know who would be an instrument of peace? (Class can give answers) Can you give me an example of someone you know who finds a way to bring love where there is hatred? (Class can give answers) Can you give me an example of someone you know who finds a way to bring pardon where there is offense? (Class can give answers) Can you give me an example of someone you know who finds a way to bring unity where there is discord? (Class can give answers) Can you give me an example of someone you know who finds a way to bring truth where there is error? (Class can give answers) Can you give me an example of someone you know who finds a way to bring faith where there is doubt? (Class can give answers) Can you give me an example of someone you know who finds a way to bring hope where there is despair? (Class can give answers) Can you give me an example of someone you know who finds a way to bring light where there is darkness? (Class can give answers) Can you give me an example of someone you know who finds a way to bring joy where there is sadness? (Class can give answers)

After this discussion use the 5-minute memory quiz to help the students memorize the last paragraph. Follow the same procedure as the 3-minute Westminster catechism memory quiz cited above. Have the group repeat the paragraph twice…remove one word…seek volunteer…have the class recite entire paragraph. Remove one word at a time and continue to repeat the exercise until the group can recite the entire paragraph without any words appearing on the board.

O Master, let me not seek as much to be consoled as to console,
to be understood as to understand, to be loved as to love, for it is in giving that one receives,
it is in self-forgetting that one finds, it is in pardoning that one is pardoned,
it is in dying that one is raised to eternal life.

We can transition to the **TOOK ACTIVITY** by telling the students that we have the privilege of participating in God's empowering/transformative process. He has revealed what His will on earth looks like. We can choose to let him empower us so we can fulfill His will, or we can choose to follow our own desires. That was essentially the choice that Adam and Eve had in the Garden of Eden.

If you chose the branch/fruit pedagogical track, you would be able to introduce the TOOK ACTIVITY in this way. Have you ever noticed that some pieces of fruit don't develop as well as others? Some pieces are larger, some smaller, some perfectly shaped and some mis-shaped. This is likely the result of the quality of the connection (stem) that the fruit/berry has to the plant. Sometimes it can be damaged by circumstances…branches swaying into one another…excessive wind or hail storms…even birds or animals can have an impact. Whatever the cause, the connection can be faulty. Fortunately, God is able to overcome every circumstance/attack that might come our way. (see Romans 8:37-39) There are times when even suffering falls within the will of God. (see John 16:33, 2 Timothy 3:12 & 1 Peter 3:17) Let's acknowledge that doing God's will on earth is not always easy. There are specific things that God has prepared for our lives. Some of them are more difficult or challenging that others.

In this matter, as in nearly every case, Jesus is our example. There were things that Jesus was destined to accomplish. The list is too long to cover in this lesson, but here are some that are specifically mentioned. You might call them Jesus' To Do List.

Matthew 16:21 NIV *From that time on Jesus began to explain to his disciples that he must go to Jerusalem and suffer many things at the hands of the elders, the chief priests and the teachers of the law, and that he must be killed and on the third day be raised to life.*

Mark 10:45 NASB "For even the Son of Man did not come to be served, but to serve, and to give his life as a ransom for many."

Luke 9:56 NASB *"For the Son of Man did not come to destroy men's lives, but to save them."* And they went on to another village.

In **John 1:29** NASB He was introduced by John the Baptist as: *the Lamb of God who takes away the sin of the world.*

In **John 4:4** NIV we found: *Now he had to go through Samaria.* He could have found another way to travel, but God had plans for the woman at the well. He had plans for that entire city.

Jesus said in **John 10:10** NASB that He *came that we may have life and have it abundantly.*

The consummate example of Jesus doing the Father's will on earth is found in **Luke 22:42** NIV when He said: *"Father, if you are willing, take this cup from me; yet not my will, but yours be done."* He then resolutely set things in motion that would lead Him to the cross. That would in turn lead to the resurrection, our redemption, His ascension to the throne of heaven, and the coming of the Holy Spirit. In our lives we can truly believe what is recorded in Philippians 2:13 NIV where it says: *For it is God who works in you to will and to act in order to fulfill his good purpose.*

God not only had a TO DO LIST for Jesus, but it is clear that He has one for each of us as well. Ephesians 2:10 NIV says: *For we are God's handiwork, created in Christ Jesus to do good works, which God prepared in advance for us to do.*

The question critical to this lesson would be: How is God's will on earth being worked out in our lives? Other than sleep and school, what are the top 5 ways that you invested your time this past week? In light of what we have learned through this lesson, how would you like to adjust your daily schedule? Let's take a little time to ask the Holy Spirit to show us some of what might be on "God's To Do" list for each of us in the coming week.

What is one way that you can adjust your free time to reflect the "To Do List" that the Holy Spirit has revealed to you?

TEACHER'S NOTE: The homework for the next two lessons will be a critical part of the upcoming lessons. Encourage the students to read (or listen to) Improvise 1 & 2 carefully in preparation for these lessons. For those that really are motivated, they could consider finding and viewing the movie Miracle (story of the U.S. Olympic hockey team in 1980).

> **Memory Verse: John 15:7-9** If you remain in me and my words remain in you, ask whatever you wish, and it will be given you. This is to my Father's glory, that you bear much fruit, showing yourselves to be my disciples. "As the Father has loved me, so have I loved you. Now remain in my love. NIV

SESSION PLANNING SHEET

Session Title: ___ Abiding – It's A Matter of Life and Death_____ Date: _____

Session Focus: _God's will for us on this earth flows from the wellspring of Jesus love and finds expression in our obedience._

Session Aims: **KNOW** _ Identify some of the things that God has clearly revealed as His will for our lives. _____

FEEL _ Express a willingness to invite the Holy Spirit to empower you so that you can do God's will._____

DO _ Invite the Spirit to reveal the ways that you might live out "God's To Do List" in the coming week. ___

Session Plan	Session Activities	Preparation
Time:__10 min__ APPROACH	**Methods, Instructions, Questions:** **Dead Plants** What are these plants lacking? Soil (nutrients), water, sunshine. What would it take to bring them back to life? **Musical line (standing version of musical chairs)** Find the place you think you deserve in this line. Find a way to convince your classmates to let you move to where you should be in the line. No pushing or shoving. When the music stops, the teacher will ask you how you got to your place in line and why you deserve to be there. **Turn line around Mark 10:45 Matthew 19:30**	**Materials:** Dead lifeless plants Teacher's choice of music Some of audio player
Time:__25 min__ BIBLE EXPLORATION	**God's Will Is As Simple As A.B.C. Rank from 1-3** TRIAD ranking groups followed by entire group ranking discussion. **ALTERNATE ACTIVITY - Blindfold 3 senses - Which fruit is this?** **Smell, Touch, and then Taste Exactly what had to happen for this "fruit" to reach maturity?** **Issue of "remaining" in the Lord"** 1. <u>R</u>emember it's His work, 2. <u>R</u>est in the Lord, 3. <u>R</u>elax…God's in control, 4. <u>R</u>evitalize by drawing upon the Spirit's power 5. leave the <u>R</u>esults with God.	Bibles, Pens or Pencils, Student Participation Study Guide or His Will As Easy as A.B.C. worksheets **BLINDFOLDS** Apple, Pear, Banana, Orange, Plum, Blueberry, Avocado, Peach, Strawberry, Rhubarb, Raisin
Time:__15 min_ LIFE IMPLICATIONS	**Memorize 1st question of the Westminster Confession in 3 minutes.** What is the chief end of man? It is to glorify God, and enjoy Him forever. **Prayer of St. Francis of Assisi – Most likely not written by him…attributed.** **Project how each element of this prayer can be enhanced through praying with and for one another.** Lord make me an instrument of your peace. Where there is hatred, let me bring love. Where there is offense, let me bring pardon. Where there is discord, let me bring union. Where there is error, let me bring truth. Where there is doubt, let me bring faith. Where there is despair, let me bring hope, where there is darkness, let me bring light, where there is sadness, let me bring joy.	White or digital board Dry erase pens, eraser **COPIES OF THE** **Prayer of St. Francis of Assisi**
Time:__10 min__ APPLICATION	**JESUS TO DO LIST…must go through Samaria…must go to Jerusalem.** **Ask Jesus what His "TO DO LIST FOR YOU" for you might be this week.** **John 15:7-9** If you remain in me and my words remain in you, ask… **Other than sleep and school, what are the top 5 ways that you invested your time this past week. As we quietly reflect on today's lesson, ask the Holy Spirit to show you some of what might be on "God's To Do list for you this week." How can you adjust your free time to reflect the "To Do List" that the Holy Spirit has revealed to you?**	

Session Planning Sheet ©2013 Dale Roy Erickson, adapted from material found in *Creative Bible Teaching* © 1998 by Lawrence O. Richards and Gary J. Bredfeldt, Moody Publishers. Used by permission.

Unit Five – Your Will Be Done On Earth As It Is In Heaven – Lesson 20 – Abiding…Prompts

We now live in a world of constant and instant accessibility…. cell phone, IPAD, Blackberry, Bluetooth, Android…etc. (these examples will probably be outdated by the time you read this, but you get the idea). Does God have your number? Do you have His?

John 15:7 If you abide in Me, and My words abide in you, you will ask what you desire, and it shall be done for you. NKJV

Abiding is not a work or a discipline. The critical factor for a branch is to stay connected to its source. God provides everything needed (nutrients, sunshine, and rain) for the branch to bear fruit. Let's stay connected to the vine.

John 15:7-9 If you remain in me and my words remain in you, ask whatever you wish, and it will be given you. This is to my Father's glory, that you bear much fruit, showing yourselves to be my disciples. "As the Father has loved me, so have I loved you. Now remain in my love. NIV

Observation tells us that many people think of prayer as an insignificant thing. If you doubt that, you should look over a person's "to do" list. While prayer should never be a daily task to be completed, it certainly has to be a daily priority.

1 Samuel 12:23 As for me, far be it from me that I should sin against the LORD by failing to pray for you. And I will teach you the way that is good and right. NIV

Every relationship begins with a conversation. Reflect back to the start of any great friendship you have ever known. Talking with that person was probably one of the best parts of your day. You'll never get to know Him without talking with Him.

1 John 5:12 He who has the Son has life; he who does not have the Son of God does not have life. NKJV

We cannot do anything in God's kingdom without His life flowing through us. A connected branch produces fruit. Anyone who spends any time in a garden, orchard or a field, understands this truth. We don't really have to be brilliant or dynamic to see God at work through our lives. We may need to be humble, prayerful, and faithful…. i.e., connected.

John 15:5 "I am the vine, you are the branches; he who abides in Me and I in him, he bears much fruit, for apart from Me you can do nothing. NKJV

Can you picture God waiting at your usual meeting place and asking, "Where are you?" He longs to meet with you.

Genesis 3:8,9 Then the man and his wife heard the sound of the LORD God as he was walking in the garden in the cool of the day, and they hid from the LORD God among the trees of the garden. But the LORD God called to the man, "Where are you?" NIV

Many people mock the idea that God will speak to us in answer to our prayers. That is true even among Christians. If you doubt this, just make the following statement and watch for the response: "God spoke to me." To disbelieve that God speaks to His people is to deny the record of His Word.

John 8:47; 10:27 He who is of God hears God's words; therefore you do not hear, because you are not of God." My sheep hear My voice, and I know them, and they follow Me. NKJV

Lesson Twenty-One: Persistence

Lesson Twenty-One is the first of three lessons which will focus on passionately and persistently bringing our prayer requests to God. Unit Six is called Give Us This Day. It invites us to approach God with assurance. The challenge presented in today's lesson will be highlighting the truth that God wants us to be persistent in our prayer life. We need to realize that the answers will come in God's time, and not necessarily according to our plans. Some of the time God will immediately bring the answer, but for His own purposes God sometimes will ask us to wait. As one of the prayer prompts assigned for this lesson says: "Unless God has already said "no," or in your heart you know that it's wrong....keep on asking.....keep on seeking....keep on knocking." This is a challenging lesson to learn for even a seasoned prayer warrior, but is even more difficult for most teenagers. There are many lessons that we all can learn from the challenge of "waiting." One important element could be the probing of the depth of our faith. Will we come to God with expectancy, persistence and perseverance? God gave Abraham the promise of a child, and the arrival would come 25 years later. Noah worked on the ark for 100 years before he ever saw the first raindrop. Israel waited for centuries in the hope of a promised Messiah. The lesson we can all learn from God's Word is that God always keeps His promises. He wants us to trust Him until His answer arrives. He wants us to trust Him even if His answer is "no" or "not at this time." Let's look at Jesus' parable in Luke 18:1-8 as the definitive illustration of this truth, but we will also buttress that with more recent illustrations and quotes.

First, let's grab the student's attention by illustrating preparation and perseverance from the U.S. Olympic hockey team from 1979-80. This team overcame what seemed to be impossible odds in order to win Olympic gold. The **HOOK ACTIVITY** for today's lesson shares YouTube videos that highlight the extreme measures (perseverance) that were involved in getting them ready for their great accomplishment. **Choose any <u>one or more</u>** of the following YouTube videos to illustrate the theme for this lesson. It should be pretty easy to illustrate the commitment, perseverance and effort involved. We will close today's lesson with the video that includes the question and answer: "Do you believe in miracles? YES!" That miracle didn't just happen, and as we look into the scriptures, we find that there is often a lot of preparation before God's miracles happen. Faith is always involved, and most often preceded by persistent prayer. Here are the locations of the videos and the catch phrases from that portion of the movie.

https://www.youtube.com/watch?v=XD6Vnynjcrc Time: 3:31   You can't be a team of common men.

Or could use this YouTube video

https://www.youtube.com/watch?v=2nR3reKPE5Y Time: 3:57 The name on the front is more important than the name on the back.

Close this portion with: "Who do you play for?" Our answer: the eternal God maker of heaven and earth.

https://www.youtube.com/watch?v=47kUqAs97-s Time: 1:31 Put your gear back on.

Close this portion with: If you think that praying is a "one and done matter," don't be surprised if God tells you to put your gear back on.

If your students would be more responsive to an animal YouTube video than sports (hockey) videos, you might choose to use the following as an introduction to the topic of persistence or perseverance.

https://www.youtube.com/watch?v=rhjBXnEFKQs Time 2:57 Bear cub following momma bear up a steep slope.

Close this portion by highlighting the attempts of the cub to chart its own path up the steep slope. Sometimes we hope the "answer to our prayers" comes from following our own path. Persevering on our own path often ends in frustration. Persisting through the direction and wisdom of God, coupled with faithful prayer, will lead to a path of satisfaction, or at the very least "escape."

We all want that miracle (promise) to arrive the minute we ask for it. Sometimes it comes that way, but God often gives us a promise, and asks us to walk that out in faith and perseverance. Do you believe in miracles? YES! Are they sometimes preceded by persistent prayer? YES! The timing of when our miracles (promises) arrive, and the manner in which they arrive, is in God's hands. God may have a for us role in pursuing a miracle. It is called persistent prayer. You can transition to the **BOOK ACTIVITY** by encouraging the students to look at what Jesus taught us about this. It is recorded in Luke 18:1-8. Let's read that over carefully at the start of our lesson.

This is not the only place where Jesus challenged us to persevere in prayer. The students should have read several passages about this in the Prayer Prompts homework. Jesus is our ultimate authority and teacher on this subject. Now that we have reviewed His parable on the topic, let's look at what some other significant people have to tell us about the importance of persistence and perseverance. Select (Circle) one of four adjectives to describe the value of each quote. Share (discuss) your thoughts with a group of three students (TRIADS). If your students have done their homework, invite them to share their thoughts as part of an entire class discussion.

QUOTES ON PERSEVERANCE AND PERSISTENCE

Nothing in the world can take the place of persistence.
Talent will not; nothing is more common than unsuccessful men with talent.
Genius will not; unrewarded genius is almost a proverb.
Education will not; the world is full of educated derelicts.
Persistence and determination alone are omnipotent.
The slogan Press On! has solved and always will solve the problems of the human race.
Calvin Coolidge

POWERFUL   STRONG   AVERAGE   WEAK

Luke 18:1 NLT One day Jesus told his disciples a story to illustrate their need for constant prayer and to show them that they must never give up.

Jesus

POWERFUL   STRONG   AVERAGE   WEAK

It's not that I'm so smart, it's just that I stay with problems longer.

Albert Einstein

POWERFUL   STRONG   AVERAGE   WEAK

Psalm 69:13 NLT But I keep right on praying to you, LORD, hoping this is the time you will show me favor. In your unfailing love, O God, answer my prayer with your sure salvation.

King David

POWERFUL   STRONG   AVERAGE   WEAK

Perseverance is the hard work you do after you get tired of doing the hard work you already did.

Newt Gingrich

POWERFUL   STRONG   AVERAGE   WEAK

Colossians 4:2,3 NASB Devote yourselves to prayer, keeping alert in it with an attitude of thanksgiving; praying at the same time for us as well, that God will open up to us a door for the word, so that we may speak forth the mystery of Christ, for which I have also been imprisoned

Apostle Paul

POWERFUL   STRONG   AVERAGE   WEAK

Many of life's failures are people who did not realize how close
they were to success when they gave up.
Thomas Edison

POWERFUL   STRONG   AVERAGE   WEAK

Micah 7:7 NIV But as for me, I watch in hope for the LORD,
I wait for God my Savior; my God will hear me.
Prophet Micah

POWERFUL   STRONG   AVERAGE   WEAK

Making your mark on the world is hard. If it were easy, everybody would do it. But it's not. It takes patience, it takes commitment, and it comes with plenty of failure along the way. The real test is not whether you avoid this failure, because you won't. It's whether you let it harden or shame you into inaction, or whether you learn from it; whether you choose to persevere.
Barack Obama

POWERFUL   STRONG   AVERAGE   WEAK

Galatians 6:9 NIV Let us not become weary in doing good, for at the proper time we will reap a harvest if we do not give up.
Apostle Paul

POWERFUL   STRONG   AVERAGE   WEAK

Faith is more powerful than government – and nothing is more powerful than God.
Donald Trump

POWERFUL   STRONG   AVERAGE   WEAK

Luke 18:7-8 NIV And will not God bring about justice for his chosen ones, who cry out to him day and night? Will he keep putting them off? I tell you, he will see that they get justice, and quickly. However, when the Son of Man comes, will he find faith on the earth?"

Jesus

POWERFUL   STRONG   AVERAGE   WEAK

With ordinary talent and extraordinary perseverance, all things are attainable.

Thomas Fowell Buxton

POWERFUL   STRONG   AVERAGE   WEAK

Hebrews 6:11 NIV   We want each of you to show this same diligence to the very end, so that what you hope for may be fully realized.

Biblical author – name unknown

POWERFUL   STRONG   AVERAGE   WEAK

A hero is an ordinary individual who finds strength to persevere
and endure in spite of overwhelming obstacles.

Christopher Reeve

POWERFUL   STRONG   AVERAGE   WEAK

Ephesians 6:18 NIV And pray in the Spirit on all occasions with all kinds of prayers and requests. With this in mind, be alert and always keep on praying for all the Lord's people.

Apostle Paul

POWERFUL   STRONG   AVERAGE   WEAK

Courage and perseverance have a magical talisman, before which difficulties disappear
and obstacles vanish into air.
John Quincy Adams

POWERFUL   STRONG   AVERAGE   WEAK

James 1:12 NIV Blessed is the one who perseveres under trial because, having stood the test, that person
will receive the crown of life that the Lord has promised to those who love him.
James – a bond servant of Christ

POWERFUL   STRONG   AVERAGE   WEAK

Let me tell you the secret that has led to my goal. My strength lies solely in my tenacity.
Louis Pasteur

POWERFUL   STRONG   AVERAGE   WEAK

2 Thessalonians 3:13 NIV And as for you, brothers and sisters, never tire of doing what is good.
Apostle Paul

POWERFUL   STRONG   AVERAGE   WEAK

If your determination is fixed, I do not counsel you to despair. Few things are impossible to
diligence and skill. Great works are performed not by strength, but perseverance.
Samuel Johnson

POWERFUL   STRONG   AVERAGE   WEAK

Psalm 27:14 _{NLT} Wait patiently for the LORD. Be brave and courageous. Yes, wait patiently for the LORD.
King David

POWERFUL   STRONG   AVERAGE   WEAK

I am convinced that about half of what separates the successful entrepreneurs from the non-successful ones is pure perseverance.
Steve Jobs

POWERFUL   STRONG   AVERAGE   WEAK

Colossians 1:11-12 _{NIV} being strengthened with all power according to his glorious might so that you may have great endurance and patience, and giving joyful thanks to the Father, who has qualified you to share in the inheritance of his holy people in the kingdom of light.
Apostle Paul

POWERFUL   STRONG   AVERAGE   WEAK

If you can't fly then run, if you can't run then walk, if you can't walk then crawl, but whatever you do you have to keep moving forward.
Martin Luther King, Jr.

POWERFUL   STRONG   AVERAGE   WEAK

Acts 1:14 _{NIV} They all joined together constantly in prayer, along with the women and Mary the mother of Jesus, and with his brothers.
Luke – A biblical author and doctor

POWERFUL   STRONG   AVERAGE   WEAK

The way to succeed is to double your failure rate.
Thomas J Watson

POWERFUL   STRONG   AVERAGE   WEAK

1 Thessalonians 5:17 _{NASB} Pray without ceasing.
Apostle Paul

POWERFUL   STRONG   AVERAGE   WEAK

Perseverance is a great element of success. If you only knock long enough
and loud enough at the gate, you are sure to wake up somebody.
Henry Wadsworth Longfellow

POWERFUL   STRONG   AVERAGE   WEAK

Luke 11:8-9 _{NASB} I tell you, even though he will not get up and give him anything because he is his
friend, yet because of his persistence he will get up and give him as much as he needs.
So I say to you, ask, and it will be given to you;
seek, and you will find; knock, and it will be opened to you.
Jesus

POWERFUL   STRONG   AVERAGE   WEAK

If you are going through hell, keep going.
Winston Churchill

POWERFUL   STRONG   AVERAGE   WEAK

James 5:11 NLT As you know, we count as blessed those who have persevered. You have heard of Job's perseverance and have seen what the Lord finally brought about. The Lord is full of compassion and mercy.

James – a bond servant of Christ

POWERFUL   STRONG   AVERAGE   WEAK

A river cuts through rock, not because of its power, but because of its persistence.

Jim Watkins

POWERFUL   STRONG   AVERAGE   WEAK

Romans 12:12 NIV Be joyful in hope, patient in affliction, faithful in prayer.

Apostle Paul

POWERFUL   STRONG   AVERAGE   WEAK

Through hard work, perseverance and a faith in God, you can live your dreams.

Ben Carson

POWERFUL   STRONG   AVERAGE   WEAK

Job 17:9 NLT The righteous keep moving forward, and those with clean hands become stronger and stronger.

Job

POWERFUL   STRONG   AVERAGE   WEAK

Instruct the students to make their best effort at selecting their favorite quote from the entire collection. If time permits, have them share why they selected that one as their favorite. We can now move to the **LOOK ACTIVITY** by highlighting the *Improvise 1 & 2* short story homework. It is one thing to agree with the Scriptures and famous people when it comes to persistence and perseverance. It is quite a different challenge to live that out in our daily experience or in a personal crisis. This might be especially challenging when it comes to persevering in our prayers.

Instruct the students to picture themselves in the place of the three main characters from the short story Improvise 1 & 2. There are two components to this exercise. There are many examples of perseverance and persistence found in this short story. Have the students highlight the most significant ones from their perspective. These questions are found in the Student Personal Study Guides.

1. Share how *perseverance* was exercised by the following characters in the story.
    a. Dave
    b. Paul
    c. Blair
2. Share how *persistence* was exercised by the following characters in the story.
    a. Dave
    b. Paul
    c. Blair

What is the best example of *perseverance* in your personal life?

What is the best example of *persistence* in your personal life?

Do you believe that Paul and Blair would have been saved without Dave's perseverance and persistent effort?

Do you believe that Paul and Blair would have been saved without their own perseverance or persistent efforts?

Take a minute to make a list of people/requests that really need a persistent prayer effort (*support*) on your part.

We will look at the special ways that God provided for the needs of these characters in our next lesson. Let the students know that we will be looking carefully into that topic in lesson 22. This should give them added motivation to read this story in their homework assignment. If they have already read this story (as instructed), they should review it again, as this will be a very important part of the next lesson.

We can close out this lesson by moving to the **TOOK ACTIVITY** using the following YouTube video: https://www.youtube.com/watch?v=F91LO5uX0yk Time: 4:09 The miracle at Lake Placid.

There are some miracles that appear to be instantaneous. Those may be simply the grace of God being applied in an individual's life. There are other miracles that follow a path of perseverant prayers. We often hear about the praying dad, mom, grandfather, grandmother, years after the miracle appears. Is there any Scripture to support this? Here is a very direct answer on that from Jesus. Mark 9:29 _{NASB} tells us: *"And He said to them, "This kind cannot come out by anything but prayer."* **Do you believe in miracles? YES!** Do you believe that the 1980 miracle win would have happened without the perseverance of the coach and the players during the months of training that preceded that game? Apply that to your prayer life in the coming year.

Ask God who you need to faithfully bring before the Lord in prayer this coming week.

MEMORY VERSE: Luke 18:1,7 Then He spoke a parable to them, that men always ought to pray and not lose heart, And will not God bring about justice for his chosen ones, who cry out to him day and night? Will he keep putting them off? _{NIV}

SESSION PLANNING SHEET

Session Title: _Persistence – Timing is Everything with God_____ Date: _____

Session Focus: _Persistent Prayer is an important element in seeing God at work through and in our lives. _____

Session Aims: **KNOW** _Identify examples of God's provision of our daily needs in response to our persistent prayers. ____

   FEEL _Acknowledge that God's answers to our faith (persistent prayers) will come in His timing not ours. _

   DO _Ask God to select certain people that He wants you to persistently prayer for this coming week. ___

Session Plan	Session Activities	Preparation
Time:__15min__ **APPROACH**	**Methods, Instructions, Questions** https://www.youtube.com/watch?v=XD6Vnynjcrc Time: 3:31 You can't be a team of common men. https://www.youtube.com/watch?v=2nR3reKPE5Y Time: 3:57 The name on the front is more important than the name on the back. Who do you play for? You play for the eternal God, Maker of heaven and earth. https://www.youtube.com/watch?v=47kUqAs97-s Time 1:31 Put your gear back on. https://www.youtube.com/watch?v=rhjBXnEFKQs Time: 2:57 Bear cub climbs mountain	**Materials** Access to YouTube Means of projection For larger groups sound amplification
Time:__20 min__ **BIBLE EXPLORATION**	**Read Luke 18:1-8 slowly and carefully.** Let's take a look at what some others have to say on the topic of perseverance and persistence. Apply these thoughts to Jesus words on prayer. **Quotes on perseverance and persistence from SPSG or Worksheet.** **Group discussion:** Which of the **quotes** on **perseverance** is the **most powerful?** Why? Which of the **quotes** on **persistence** is the **most powerful?** Why?	Bibles, Student Participation Study Guides, Pens or Pencils Or Quotes on perseverance and Persistence worksheets Pens, pencils or markers
Time:__15 min__ **LIFE IMPLICATIONS**	Examples of *perseverance* from Improvise 1 &2 Dave Paul Blair Examples of *persistence* from Improvise 1 & 2 Dave Paul Blair Best example of *perseverance* in your personal life thus far. Best example of *persistence* in your personal life thus far. Make a list of people/requests that really need a persistent prayer effort.	
Time:__10 min__ **APPLICATION**	https://www.youtube.com/watch?v=F91LO5uX0yk **Time: 4:09 Miracle at Lake Placid** There are some miracles that appear to be instantaneous. There are other miracles that follow a path of perseverant prayers. We often hear about the praying dad, mom, grandfather, grandmother, years after the miracle appears. Is there any Scripture to support this? Here is a very direct answer on that from Jesus is found in Mark 9:29. **Do you believe in miracles? YES!** Do you believe that the 1980 miracle win would have happened without the perseverance of the coach, and the players? Let's apply that to our prayer lives in the coming year. **Ask God who He might want on your prayer list this week.**	Access to YouTube Means of projection For larger groups sound amplification

Unless God has already said "no," or in your heart you know that it's wrong....keep on asking.....keep on seeking....keep on knocking.

Matthew 7:7,8 "Ask and it will be given to you; seek and you will find; knock and the door will be opened to you. For everyone who asks receives; he who seeks finds; and to him who knocks, the door will be opened" _{NLT}

The difference between persistent prayer and nagging God is found in the tone. One is the joy of constant communion and the other is the faithless repetition of a selfish request. Every parent, brother, sister or even babysitter knows the distinction.

Psalm 88:1,2 O Lord, God of my salvation, I have cried out day and night before You. Let my prayer come before You; Incline Your ear to my cry. _{NKJV}

Here's an interesting "life goal." I want to be remembered as someone who worked hard in prayer to make sure that others become mature in Christ.

Colossians 4:12 Epaphras, from your city, a servant of Christ Jesus, sends you his greetings. He always prays earnestly for you, asking God to make you strong and perfect, fully confident of the whole will of God. _{NLT}

The persistent flow of water can be incredibly destructive. A leaky water pipe can destroy roads, or the foundations of a home. A persistent flow of water can be incredibly constructive. A hydroelectric generator can create electricity. God, help our persistent prayers to have a constructive rather than a destructive nature.

Luke 18:1,7 Then He spoke a parable to them, that men always ought to pray and not lose heart, And will not God bring about justice for his chosen ones, who cry out to him day and night? Will he keep putting them off? _{NIV}

Some doors are locked and will remain so until we find the right key. Pressing on with a key that doesn't fit is futile. Once we find the key that matches the lock, we will proceed through an open door. Devote yourself to prayer.

Colossians 4:2,3 Devote yourselves to prayer, keeping alert in it with an attitude of thanksgiving; praying at the same time for us as well, that God will open up to us a door for the word, so that we may speak forth the mystery of Christ, for which I have also been imprisoned _{NASB}

Effective prayer is in some ways like being in a marathon. Jesus is a friend shouting words of encouragement.

Luke 18:1 One day Jesus told his disciples a story to illustrate their need for constant prayer and to show them that they must never give up _{NLT}

There are a lot of frustrations that might tempt us to "give up" on prayer. Keep on keeping on. You will surely reap the reward of God's favor in His time.

Psalm 69:13 But I keep right on praying to you, LORD, hoping this is the time you will show me favor. In your unfailing love, O God, answer my prayer with your sure salvation. _{NLT}

Lesson Twenty-Two: Petition/Provision

Lesson Twenty-Two is the second of three lessons which will focus on passionately and persistently bringing our prayer requests to God. Unit Six is called Give Us This Day. It invites us to approach God with assurance. Today's lesson is about God making provision for our needs. We have already looked at "faith" in a previous lesson, so we won't cover that ground again. It is assumed that faith will be a critical issue when we bring our petitions to God. One of the elements we will feature in this lesson is that God knows what we need. He is willing and able to meet those needs. When we are able to look back on the events of our lives, we often see that God was making advance preparations for our needs. It is a "faith building" exercise to reflect upon God's faithfulness in past events/challenges. God often told His people to set up markers to help them remember His miraculous provision. A good example of this would be the stones that God had them remove from the Jordon River after He stopped the water so they could cross. Joshua chapter 4:21-24 NLT records it this way: *Then Joshua said to the Israelites, "In the future your children will ask, 'What do these stones mean?' Then you can tell them, 'This is where the Israelites crossed the Jordan on dry ground.' For the LORD your God dried up the river right before your eyes, and he kept it dry until you were all across, just as he did at the Red Sea when he dried it up until we had all crossed over. He did this so all the nations of the earth might know that the LORD's hand is powerful, and so you might fear the LORD your God forever."*

We are going to use the **Improvise 1 & 2** short story as an example of advance preparation which aids in a rescue effort. This story is a perfect illustration of God's heart in making advance preparation for our needs. The most critical of those needs would be salvation (which is clearly laid out in this story) and our need of the Holy Spirit which Jesus' parable in Luke 11:1-13 demonstrates. We can easily focus our prayers for the provision of earthly needs (our daily bread). Clearly, God has invited us to ask for those things, but Jesus was always pointing his disciples to the greater need. That would be our need for divine power (the Holy Spirit within us) and our eternal destiny (salvation). Let's keep our focus on these crucial needs, and appreciate the heart of the Giver.

We will start off this lesson with a brief YouTube clip. You can find this at: https://www.youtube.com/watch?v=OHc8ZjiSqCQ. It is an advance trailer for the movie The Mountain Between Us. This trailer is a great setup for the Rescue Provisions Exercise which was a part of homework (in the Student Personal Study Guide and the short story **Improvise 1 &2**).

We will use this as the **HOOK ACTIVITY** in order to draw their attention to the advance provisions that God makes for our needs. Draw them into today's topic by asking these questions:

If you were sent on this rescue mission, what would you take with you?

If you were waiting to be rescued, what would you hope was already available in the plane?

What does God provide for you on a daily basis that is vital to your earthly existence?

What does God provide for you that is vital to your future destiny?

Make the transition to the **BOOK ACTIVITY** by saying that we will spend some time in today's lesson learning about the critical things that God has provided...is providing...and will provide to meet our needs. This is clearly taught in Luke 11:1-13. One of Jesus' disciples asked Him to teach them to pray just as John had taught his disciples. Jesus responded with what we now call the Lord's prayer, and immediately followed that template prayer with a parable about a persistent friend. This friend kept on asking/knocking until he received what he was looking for. This parable was not only about persistence (which we covered in the last lesson), but also about the expected response. It is quite easy when reflecting on this passage (Luke 11:1-13) to look right past the critical point being made. Jesus' primary focus was on the heart of the giver. Luke 11:13 $_{NLT}$ relates the crux of the matter when it concludes the parable like this: *"So if you sinful people know how to give good gifts to your children, how much more will your heavenly Father give the Holy Spirit to those who ask him."* Make sure that the students are reminded of this point throughout today's lesson.

As an illustration of God's provision, we are going to use the short story Improvise 1 & 2. If the students have the Student Personal Study Guides, invite them to turn to the RESCUE PROVISIONS exercise in lesson 22. If they don't have the study guides, you can run off copies of the exercise from the Teacher's Resource CD. It is assumed that in many settings there will be some students who have done their homework, and some that were not as faithful. Divide the group into sets of three (TRIADS - 1 student who regularly does their homework and others who may or may not be as well prepared). Have them compete to see who can find the missing vowels in this exercise. When they are done, share a brief synopsis of why this item was vital in the rescue effort. The critical facet will be the impact that the wind (God's provision) had on this rescue. We often overlook God's hand of provision during our most challenging moments. Like the Jordon River memorial stones, your students may need some markers (stories) of God's past provision to help them face existing challenges.

Answers in the order given in the Rescue Provision Exercise:

Light substantial Jacket, Gor-Tex coveralls & gloves, medical supplies, Advil/ Vicodin, air splint, cervical collar, food, canned meat, fruit, energy bars, water, rope, electronic locator, small tent, signal flares. plastic tarp, blankets, warm clothing, head band with LED light, duct tape, bone saw, Leatherman multi-tool, knife, handgun, Baklava, rubber coat, rubber pants, touque, sleeping bags, seats of the plane, wing of the plane, seat belts, wool blankets, loose baggage, transmitter beacon, changed position of the plane, brought battery back to life, made exit easier, provided insulation, protected pilot's body from predators

After a summary of how the advance preparations, existing provisions, and God's intervention, are critical to the rescue effort, we can then move to the **LOOK ACTIVITY**. It is one thing to make daily requests, but it is also important to utilize whatever provisions are at hand. It is wonderful when God immediately intervenes on our behalf, but it is critically important to press on with our requests when the answer doesn't come that quickly. The question which naturally arises would be: "How do these elements coalesce in answer to our prayers?" How can we distinguish the prayers that we "must persist in bringing" from those where God's answer is "no," or "not at this time?" When do we need to jump in and use our own efforts (improvise) to bring about change, and how does that relate to pressing on with our requests? We might get some help from the following Reflection Point.

REFLECTION POINT

Written in the front page of Dr. David Jeremiah's Bible

When you pray, if the *REQUEST* is wrong, God says "<u>NO</u>."

When you pray, if the *TIMING* is wrong, God says: "<u>SLOW</u>."

When you pray, if you need to *FIX SOMETHING IN YOUR LIFE,* God says "<u>GROW</u>."

If the *REQUEST* is right, and the *TIMING* is right and *YOU* are right, God says "<u>GO</u>."

Choose from the four possible answers to prayer listed in the Reflection Point. Read the passages that are listed below and assign which word would best describe God's answer to that person's request. Select from these choices WRONG REQUEST, TIMING'S NOT RIGHT, FIX SOMETHING, OR YOU GOT IT. It is possible that more than one selection could be correct.

Acts 16:6-14; 19:21-22; 2 Corinthians 1:15-20 Paul __NOT AT THIS TIME_____

Matthew 17:14-21 Disciples ___FIX SOMETHING_____

1 Chronicles 28:2-6, 29:10-19 David ____WRONG REQUEST_____

Esther 3:13-5:8, 6:14-7:6 Esther ___NOT AT THIS TIME/YOU GOT IT_____

Judges 6:11-16,36-40; 7:2-14 Gideon ___YOU GOT IT_____

Deuteronomy 3:23-28 Moses ____WRONG REQUEST_____

1 Samuel 23:1-5, 2 Samuel 5:17-25 David ____YOU GOT IT_____

Luke 2:25-38 Simeon, Anna _____YOU GOT IT_____

We will want to wrap up this lesson with two main points. For the **TOOK ACTIVITY** we will invite the learners to thank God for His provision. One of the primary means of provision that God will use in their lives is their parents and/or others who serve in a similar capacity. We will also challenge them to actually ASK for the Father's provision. In today's passage that provision is clearly identified as the Holy Spirit.

THANK YOU NOTE EXERCISE

Write a thank you note to your parents (and/or other providers) for things that they provide for you on a regular basis.

Write a thank you note to God for all the things that He has provided. Make a list of the things for which you are most grateful. On the back of the note, make a list of things that you believe that God will provide for you in the future.

The Scripture we have focused on today (Luke 11:1-13) is clear. The Father is more than willing to give the Holy Spirit to those who ASK. Invite the class to invite the Holy Spirit to come into their lives, and watch how God responds. Romans 8:9 NLT says: *But you are not controlled by your sinful nature. You are controlled by the Spirit if you have the Spirit of God living in you. (And remember that those who do not have the Spirit of Christ living in them do not belong to him at all.)* According to 2 Corinthians 5:17 NLT that makes a new life possible. It says: *This means that anyone who belongs to Christ has become a new person. The old life is gone; a new life has begun!* The Father is more than willing if we ask Him. Let's do that now.

MEMORY VERSE: Philippians 4:6 NLT Don't worry about anything; instead, pray about everything. Tell God what you need, and thank him for all he has done.

SESSION PLANNING SHEET

Session Title: __Petition/Provision God knows what you need even before you ask._____ Date: _____

Session Focus: _God has promised to meet all of our needs and sometimes the provision comes in unexpected ways. ____

Session Aims: **KNOW** _ Identify the greatest needs that God has made provision for in our lives. _____

FEEL _ Express confidence that God knows what your needs are and will provide for them. _____

DO _ Write a Thank You card to your parents (or others) and God for their daily provision in your life. _

Session Plan	Session Activities	Preparation
Time:__15min__ **APPROACH**	**Methods, Instructions, Questions** **https://www.youtube.com/watch?v=OHc8ZjiSqCQ** Start when plane warning signal begins at about 32 second point…continue until about 1 min 55 sec point when he says: "We aren't going to die…not today." If you were sent on this rescue mission, what would you take with you? If you were waiting to be rescued, what would you hope was already available in the plane? What does God provide for you on a daily basis that is vital to your earthly existence? (see Luke 11:1-13) What does God provide for you that is vital to your future destiny?	**Materials** Computer screen or means of projection, Audio, YouTube access
Time:__20 min__ **BIBLE EXPLORATION**	**RESCUE PROVISIONS EXERCISE** **Divide the class into TRIADS** Light substantial jacket, Gor-Tex coveralls & gloves, medical supplies, Advil/Vicodin, air splint, cervical collar, food, canned meat, fruit, energy bars, water, rope, electronic locator, small tent, signal flares, plastic tarp, blankets, warm clothing, head band with LED light, duct tape, bone saw, Leatherman multi-tool, knife, handgun, Baklava, rubber coat, rubber pants, touque, sleeping bags, seats of the plane, wing of the plane, seat belts, wool blankets, loose baggage, transmitter beacon, changed position of the plane, brought battery back to life, made exit easier, provided insulation, protected pilot's body from predators What are some things your parents, or other people, provide on a regular basis? What are some things that God provides for you on a regular basis? What are some things that you ask God to provide on a regular basis?	Kingdom Builders SPSG or RESCUE PROVISIONS EXERCISE Worksheet, Pens or pencils
Time:__15 min___ **LIFE IMPLICATIONS**	**REFLECTION POINT** David Jeremiah quote on front page of his Bible When you pray, if the request is wrong God says "no." When you pray, if the timing is wrong God says "wait." When you pray, if you need to fix something in your life God says "grow." If the request is right, and the timing is right, and you are right, God says "go." What do you believe was God's answer in the following situations? Acts 16:6-14, 19:21-22; 2 Corinthians 1:15-20; Paul, Matthew 17:14-21 Disciples, 1 Chronicles 28:2-6, 29:10-19 David, Esther 3:13-5:8, 6:14-7:6 Esther Judges 6:11-16, 36-40; 7:2-14 Gideon Deuteronomy 3:23-28 Moses, 1 Samuel 23:1-5, 2 Samuel 5:17-25 David Luke 2:25-38 Simeon, Anna	Kingdom Builders SPSG or Reflection Point posted on a white or digital board, dry erase pens, eraser
Time:__10 min__ **APPLICATION**	**THANK YOU NOTE EXERCISE** Write a thank you note to your parents (or other providers) for things that they provide for you on a regular basis. Write a thank you note to God for all the things that He has provided for you. List the things for which you are most grateful. On the back of the note, list the things that you believe that God will provide for you in the future. The Scripture we focused on today (Luke 11:1-13) is clear. The Father is more than willing to give the Holy Spirit to those who ASK. Challenge the class to invite the Holy Spirit to come into their lives, and watch how God responds. That will make an entirely NEW LIFE possible for each of us.	Thank You note cards Pens or pencils

One of the provisions that God has made for stress/worry/anxiety is prayer.

Philippians 4:6   Be anxious for nothing, but in everything by prayer and supplication, with thanksgiving, let your requests be made known to God   NKJV

Prayer certainly has a private side, but it warms the heart to hear that we are being prayed for on a regular basis.

Ephesians 1:16   I have never stopped thanking God for you. I pray for you constantly   NLT

Are we living in the "real" world?   In the "real" world life is short.   In the "real" world a baby looks to their father and mother to provide.   In the "real" world God takes care of every vital need his children might have.   I want to live in the "real" world.

Luke 12:27,28   Consider the lilies, how they grow: they neither toil nor spin; and yet I say to you, even Solomon in all his glory was not arrayed like one of these.   If then God so clothes the grass, which today is in the field and tomorrow is thrown into the oven, how much more will He clothe you, O you of little faith?   NKJV

We have been directed by God to intercede for the government officials that He has placed in positions of responsibility and authority.

1 Timothy 2:1,2   First of all, then, I urge that entreaties and prayers, petitions and thanksgivings, be made on behalf of all men, for kings and all who are in authority, so that we may lead a tranquil and quiet life in all godliness and dignity.   NASB

The following statement should be our default setting when we come to prayer.   If He chooses to say "no" or "wait," it is always for the best.

Matthew 7:11   If you then, being evil, know how to give good gifts to your children, how much more will your Father who is in heaven give good things to those who ask Him!   NKJV

AFTER THEY PRAYED (it's amazing how easily we gloss over that), incredible supernatural things began to happen.

Acts 4:31   After they prayed, the place where they were meeting was shaken. And they were all filled with the Holy Spirit and spoke the word of God boldly.   NIV

Luke 3:21   Now when all the people were baptized, Jesus was also baptized, and while He was praying, heaven was opened   NASB

We aren't instructed to pray for tomorrow's provision or next year's provision.   We are instructed to ask God to give us our daily bread.   You would almost think that we are invited to a place of daily dependence upon God.   That's exactly what God intended from the very start.

Luke 11:3   Give us day by day our daily bread   NKJV

Lesson Twenty-Three: Shelter

Lesson Twenty-Three is the third of three lessons which will focus on God's provision in our lives. The theme of today's lesson could easily be summarized by reflecting upon Psalm 18:1-3 which says: *"I will love You, O LORD, my strength. The LORD is my rock and my fortress and my deliverer; My God, my strength, in whom I will trust; My shield and the horn of my salvation, my stronghold. I will call upon the LORD, who is worthy to be praised; So shall I be saved from my enemies."* NKJV Prayer is a key element of seeking shelter from God. This might be assumed, but could be overlooked in our daily practice or heart attitude. In order to quickly build the case for the place of prayer in God's provision of shelter, we will review some of the Psalms that support this concept. There are two elements which we will feature in these verses. First, crying out to the Lord…i.e. praying. And second, God's response as our Protector. I strongly encourage each teacher to read through these references in preparation for teaching this lesson. The verses that have been highlighted with a bold and/or underlined text are the clearest examples in support of the two themes. Psalms 3:**3-5**; 4:**1**; 5:**1-3,11-12**; 6:**8-10**; 7:**1,10,11**; 9:9,10,**13**; 10:**12,17-18**; 12:**1**,**5**; 13:3,4; 16:**1**,**8**; 17:**1**,**6-8**; 18:1-3,**19**; 20:**1**,6,9; 21:**2**-3; 22:**5**,**24**; 25:**1-3**; 26:1,12; 27:**5**,**7-8**,**13**; 28:**1-2**,**6-8**; 30:**2**,**8**,**10-11**; 31:**1-3**,*15*-17,19-**20**; 32:**6-7**; 33:13,18-**20**; 34:**4-7**,**15**,*17-19*,**22**; 35:1-2,**10**,26; 36:7-8; 37:25,**39-40**; 38:15-16,21-22; 39:7,**12**-13; 40:**1-3**, 11-13,**17**; 41:1-3, 10-11; 42:9,11;43:5; 44:24,26; 46:**1**,10-11, 49:15; 50:**15**; 51:1; 52:7-9; 54:**1-2,4,7**; 55:**1-2**,**16-18**,**22**; 56:9,**13**; 57:**1-3**; 58:11; 59:**1**,9,**16-17**; 60:5,12; 61:**1-4**; 62:2,**6-8**; 63:7; 64:**10**; 65:**2**; 66:12,**17-20**; 68:**19-20**,69:**13-18**,29,33; 70:**5**; 71:**1-4**,20-22; 72:**4**,**12-14** (King David is acting here, but God's actions may be implied). We will stop at Psalm 72:20 which says: the prayers of David are ended.

For the **HOOK ACTIVITY** in this lesson we will use a unique version of the lost and found game. Separate the group into boys and girls. Have each group select one person who will be the first to hide. That person will receive specific instructions that they are to hide in a location on the facility or grounds where others can join them and the group can still be well hidden. Allow time for the first guy and first girl to find a hiding place. Instruct the remaining group that they are to look for the person designated to hide from their group (gender). When they find them, they are to silently remain with them in hiding until they hear the siren indicating the activity is over. Each person that found their way to the group receives a small reward when the activity is over. You can transition out of the Hook Activity by suggesting that there are many reasons that people choose to go into hiding. Often, they are looking for a place of safety. This could be looking for safety emotionally, physically, spiritually, or in other ways. Today we will look at some of the reasons that people are looking for a place of safety and protection from bullying and abuse. We will also look at some of the motivations behind bullying/abuse, and the motivations that God would desire to see in our lives.

Move to the **BOOK ACTIVITY** by suggesting that there are many Biblical examples of people who either suffered from or created a bullying/abuse situation. We will look at some of these examples and search for the correct response for the people involved.

BULLYING/ABUSE WORD PUZZLE

Bullying and abuse are very similar in nature. See if you can find the following types of abuse in the word puzzle and then match them to the examples found in the Scriptures that follow on the next page. We will learn that creating these abuses/bullying situations is always wrong, but it appears that even good people have been subjected to such things. To suffer from these kinds of experiences is not something God's desires for us, but a horrible expression of a sinful humanity. Obviously, there was no cyber bullying in Scriptural time, but we will use an example of harassment as an illustration of cyber bullying.

VERBAL	PHYSICAL	RACIAL
CHILD	CYBER (harassment)	SIBLING
POWER	SEXUAL	SPOUSAL

S	P	O	U	S	A	L	Z	G	H	S	G	R	U	I
V	X	P	J	X	P	P	N	K	E	Y	B	E	M	F
M	E	A	K	L	H	I	L	X	D	S	W	W	S	Z
V	R	R	H	S	L	U	U	O	Q	L	A	O	S	I
A	Y	Y	B	B	X	A	Q	K	X	F	I	P	L	D
L	U	Q	I	A	L	D	R	E	B	Y	C	H	L	W
A	M	S	M	Q	L	T	Z	X	E	D	C	Z	C	R
C	R	P	E	U	R	U	F	W	W	W	Y	Z	S	B
I	A	U	U	V	N	D	T	G	Q	A	P	K	G	Y
S	C	R	U	K	X	W	L	E	S	K	B	U	Q	I
Y	I	D	D	G	Y	J	H	I	N	O	K	J	J	G
H	A	Y	D	C	F	Z	L	C	T	X	F	J	L	H
P	L	V	O	D	Z	U	A	B	N	J	P	J	W	Y
F	S	F	A	A	K	B	B	N	K	S	D	E	Y	Y
E	D	C	T	E	G	V	P	T	J	D	V	B	X	N

The love motivation is the ideal for us on the personal level. There are other motivations and responsibilities in response to bullying/abuse. The motivation to protect the abused is a correct response for you, for friends, for authorities and others. Finding a way to withdraw (seek shelter) from a bullying or abusive situation is generally a good start. That is not always possible or easily done. A person and/or an agency may be able to find a reasonable means of confronting the destruction behavior. Appealing to a person of authority for protection and/or support, both personal and legal, is also an option. While there are many options available, we should always realize that our best refuge and first choice is God. We can call out to Him for shelter, protection, justice and support. We can also pray that God might intervene for us, for the perpetrator, and any others who might be involved in the situation.

Match a type of abuse/bullying found in the word puzzle with the following Scriptures. Based on what we learned from 1 Corinthians 13, what would your prayer or course of action look like in this Scriptural example? How did God respond, or how would God likely respond in those situations. Some categories will fit in more than one Scriptural passage.

Luke 11:14–22; 12:1-7__Verbal (could also fit Cyber/harassment or Power) _____

Prayer for or action towards the abuser. _ Jesus publicly challenged them with logic and declaring the truth. _____

_____

Prayer for or action towards the abused. _ Words of encouragement stating that God hears what is being said (whispered), and is looking out for the abused. _____

_____

What are some of God's responses to the bullying/abuse? __ God sees (hears) what is being done and wants the abused to know that He cares. The hidden or overt abuse will be revealed and dealt with in God's time and in God's way. _____

_____

Genesis 12:11-19 __Spousal_____

Prayer for or action towards the abuser. __ In this case the abused submitted to her husband. This may or may not be the right course depending upon the nature of the threat. At times withdrawal might be your best option. _____

_____

Prayer for or action towards the abused. __ God watched over the abused person (Sarah) by providing warnings and protective guards against abuse. _____

_____

What are some of God's responses to the bullying/abuse? __ In this case God prevented the actions of potential abuse from happening. _____

Mark 14:32-36,64-65; Luke 23:33-34 __Physical (could also fit Cyber/harassment or Power)____

Prayer for or action towards the abuser. __ Jesus prayed that they would be forgiven. _____

Prayer for or action towards the abused. _Jesus asked his friends to pray for him in His struggle, and submitted to God's will after asking the Father to remove this cup from him. _____

What are some of God's responses to the bullying/abuse? __ God did not prevent the abuse, but allowed it for the greater good of bringing deliverance from sin to the world. In answer to Jesus' prayer, God offers forgiveness to all those who sincerely ask for it. _____

John 4:4,9-10,25-29 ___Racial_____

Prayer for or action towards the abuser. __ Jesus stepped in to overcome the prejudice through personal action. He set the right example by not acquiescing to the existing racial prejudice. _____

Prayer for or action towards the abused. _ Rather than accept the existing prejudices, Jesus took actions that challenged the status quo. He confronted the fallacies of the racial thinking. _____

What are some of God's responses to the bullying/abuse? __ Purposely traveled to the source of the problem (both personal and societal). He provided a grace filled encounter. _____

---

1 Samuel 1:6-7,10,15-18 ___Cyber (Harassment)_____

Prayer for or action towards the abuser. _ Husband showed kindness to the abused. He should have provided more protection for the abused person. _____

Prayer for or action towards the abused. _ Hannah took her brokenness to the Lord and asked for a remedy. _____

_____

What are some of God's responses to the bullying/abuse? __ God heard her cry for relief and answered her prayers to relieve her distress. _____

_____

Genesis 37:18-24,28-29; 39:1-5,21; 40:14-15; 42:6-8,28,31-34; 50:20-21 ___Sibling____

Prayer for or action towards the abuser. _The motivations of the abusers were tested to see if their hearts had changed. (Gen 42:28,31-34) _____

_____

Prayer for or action towards the abused. _ Joseph's integrity was tested and proven multiple times. Joseph asserted his innocence and asked for relief. (Gen. 40:14-15) _____

_____

What are some of God's responses to the bullying/abuse? _ God caused Joseph to prosper even while in slavery and imprisonment. God allowed Joseph to be in a position of authority which tested Joseph's and his brother's motivations. They all passed the test and relationships were restored. _____

_____

2 Samuel 13:11-12,20-21; 18:14-15,33 ___Sexual (could also fit Sibling, Child or Power) _____

Prayer for or action towards the abuser _His brother (Absalom) covered up the abuse and later paid for these actions. _____

_____

Prayer for or action towards the abused. ____ His father (David) was angry but did nothing and later paid for these actions. _____

_____

What are some of God's responses to the bullying/abuse? _Amnon was killed by Absalom, Absalom was killed by David's military leader. David lost both sons because he was unwilling to confront sin. _____

_____

1 Samuel 19:1-2,10-12,18; 20:15-17; 23:16; 2 Samuel 5:1-4 ___Power (could also fit Physical) ____

Prayer for or action towards the abuser _ David fled and told a spiritual authority what Saul had done. ____

Prayer for or action towards the abused. _ Jonathan warned David - provided a means for escape, Michal provided a means for escape. _____

What are some of God's responses to the bullying/abuse? __God provided a dear friend in Jonathan and provided a means of escape, David anointed as king in Saul's place. _____

2 Samuel 11:1-5; 12:7-13,24-25 __Sexual (could also fit Power)_____

Prayer for or action towards the abuser. _ There were multiple public consequences for this sin. David's family and military leaders turned against him. The baby from this abuse died. God's reputation was tarnished. _____

Prayer for or action towards the abused. _ God gave Bathsheba a son who became a great king (Jedidiah – meaning beloved of the Lord…later called Solomon). _____

What are some of God's responses to the bullying/abuse? _ God declared that the sin which was done by David in secret would be done against David in public and his own family would turn against him. _____

We can now move to the **LOOK ACTIVITY** to review how much we all need supernatural help to change the patterns created by bullying/abusive behaviors. Every day we need the Spirit's help in shaping our hearts toward the right motivations. We need to be transformed and see the fruit of the Spirit flowing from our lives. We can set goals and resolutions to improve our responses to others, but we are likely to fail without a changed heart.

That will also be true for the person who we would define as a bully or abuser.

As you think about your past week, which of the love motivations were most challenging for you? Which were the most challenging for other people involved in a bullying/abuse situation?

In considering the motivations behind bullying and/or abuse, we might look at how love is described in 1 Corinthians 13:4-7 and then write what the opposite motivation might look like.

LOVE is patient   BULLYING/ABUSE is ___irate, agitated, frustrated, intolerant ___

LOVE is kind   BULLYING/ABUSE is _bitter, cruel, angry, mean, inconsiderate _

LOVE is **not** jealous   BULLYING/ABUSE is _jealous, discontented, self-satisfied _____

LOVE does **not** brag   BULLYING/ABUSE is **not** _ humble, modest, meek, reserved ___

LOVE is **not** arrogant   BULLYING/ABUSE is _conceited, haughty, boastful, brazen ____

LOVE does **not** act unbecomingly   BULLYING/ABUSE is **not** _ proper, suitable, decent, gracious __

LOVE does **not** seek its own   BULLYING/ABUSE is _uncaring, greedy, thoughtless, brutal___

LOVE is **not** provoked   BULLYING/ABUSE does **not** _appease, placate, help, calm_____

LOVE does **not** take into account   BULLYING/ABUSE is _unforgiving, ungracious, unmerciful___
a wrong *suffered*

LOVE does **not** rejoice   BULLYING/ABUSE is _dishonorable, unfair, unjust, immoral___
in unrighteousness

LOVE rejoices with the truth   BULLYING/ABUSE is _dishonest, deceitful, devious, disloyal___

LOVE bears all things   BULLYING/ABUSE is _unsupportive, hurtful, injurious, wounds_

LOVE believes all things   BULLYING/ABUSE _doubts, suspects, infers, judges__all things

LOVE hopes all things   BULLYING/ABUSE _presumes, fears, distrusts _____ all things

LOVE endures all things   BULLYING/ABUSE _undermines, rejects, resists_____ all things

As we move to the **TOOK ACTIVITY**, we should have the students ask God if there is any way they could have hurt someone this past week. Ask God if there is anything they need to do to make things right in that instance.

Look over the Love/Bullying/Abuse worksheet and review how you might best pray for or respond to someone who may have hurt you in the past.

If there has been bullying/abuse in your life, take time right now to prepare a plan of action based upon what you have learned today. Include possible resources, prayers or personal response. Feel free to seek help from the teacher, parent, a school counselor, pastor or other authority.

With God's help make a commitment to pray for or respond properly to that person in the coming week.

MEMORY VERSE: 2 Corinthians 1:11 He will rescue us because you are helping by praying for us. As a result, many will give thanks to God because so many people's prayers for our safety have been answered. **NLT**

SESSION PLANNING SHEET

Session Title: _ Shelter – Protection from the Storms of Life_____ Date: _____

Session Focus: _ Recognize that God is a shelter in the storms of life. Our prayers provide deliverance for us and others. __

Session Aims: **KNOW** _ Identify some of the potential storms we might face, and share the possible means of protection._

FEEL _ Express confidence that God will provide protection, and/or provide a means of escape. _____

DO _ Prepare a personal plan of action in seeking refuge from the storms of life. _____

Session Plan	Session Activities	Preparation
Time:__15min__ **APPROACH**	**Methods, Instructions, Questions** **Hide and Seek Sardines** One person from each gender is selected to find a hiding place (boys find boys – girls find girls). Each person who finds the hidden person from their group has to join them in hiding. They have to remain hidden until the horn blows. Everyone who finds the hiding place and remains hidden gets a reward. Those people who cannot find the hidden group are not rewarded. One of the keys to this exercise is that the hiding place must be large enough to keep the full group hidden.	**Materials** Rewards for the group that finds the hidden person and remains in the group that is in hiding
Time: __20 min__ **BIBLE EXPLORATION**	**Bullying/Abuse Word Puzzle** Find the 9 categories of bullying/abuse in the word puzzle. Answer the following questions associated with those categories after reading the Scriptural examples (may have been done for student guide homework). **Prayer for or action towards the abuser.** **Prayer for or action towards the abused.** **What are some of God's responses to the bullying/abuse?** If time permits discuss the answers the students provide.	Student Participation Study Guides OR Bullying Abuse Word Puzzles worksheets Pens/Pencils, Bibles
Time:__15 min___ **LIFE IMPLICATIONS**	**Love verses Bullying Abuse Motivations worksheet** **1 Corinthians 13:4-7 and antonyms (or opposite motivations)** Every day we need the Spirit's help in moving our hearts in the right direction. We need to be transformed and see the fruit of the Spirit flowing from our lives. We can set goals and resolutions to improve our responses to others, but we are likely to fail without a changed heart. That is also true for the person we would define as a bully or abuser. As you think about your past week, which of the love motivations was most challenging? Greatest challenge for those facing bullying/abuse?	Love/Bullying/Abuse Motivations Worksheet Pens, Bibles
Time:__10 min__ **APPLICATION**	Ask God if there is any way your failure to have a perfect love motivation might have hurt someone this past week. Ask God if there is anything you need to do to make things right in that instance. Look over the Love/Bullying/Abuse worksheet and review how you might best pray for or respond to someone who may have hurt you in the past. **If there has been bullying/abuse in your life, take time right now to prepare a plan of action based upon what you have learned today.** **Include resources/prayer/response.** With God's help, make a commitment to pray for and respond properly to that person this week.	Provide names/phone numbers for local pastors who have experience counseling abuse victims Provide local resource materials for Abuse/Bullying Counseling and similar agencies

Session Planning Sheet ©2013 Dale Roy Erickson, adapted from material found in *Creative Bible Teaching* © 1998 by Lawrence O. Richards and Gary J. Bredfeldt, Moody Publishers. Used by permission.

Unit Six – Give Us This Day Our Daily Bread – Lesson 23 – Shelter…Prompts

When our hearts are crushed, we are inclined to believe that our prayers are going unheard. Nothing is further from the truth.

Psalm 34:18 The LORD is near to the brokenhearted, and saves those who are crushed in spirit. ₙₐₛ_b NASB

The beauty of a cell phone is that we can reach out for help from almost anywhere. The exception would be when we travel into an area where we don't have coverage. Thank God that when we need help our connection will never be dropped….at least not from His end.

Psalm 4:1 Answer me when I call, O God of my righteousness! You have relieved me in my distress; Be gracious to me and hear my prayer. NLT

To suggest the Christian life doesn't have mountain tops and valleys denies reality. One of the best ways to face them both is to walk with the One who created them.

Psalm 28:7 The Lord is my strength and my shield; My heart trusted in Him, and I am helped; Therefore my heart greatly rejoices, And with my song I will praise Him NKJV

If you see a tornado coming, you should get in a bunker and wait until the storm has passed. God, you are my refuge in times of trouble.

Psalm 62:5-8 My soul, wait silently for God alone, For my expectation is from Him. He only is my rock and my salvation; He is my defense; I shall not be moved. In God is my salvation and my glory; The rock of my strength, And my refuge, is in God. Trust in Him at all times, you people; Pour out your heart before Him; God is a refuge for us. Selah NIV

I don't have to go looking for trouble. It finds me without anyone's help. I need directions to a place where I can escape from trouble. If you are in a place where you think: "I haven't got a hope." Just look up!

Psalm 32:7 You are my hiding place; You shall preserve me from trouble; You shall surround me with songs of deliverance. Selah NKJV

Distraction and doubt cripple our prayers. They come rushing in when life is difficult. Reflecting upon what is true will provide shelter and strength for the storms of life.

Deuteronomy 32:4 He is the Rock, His work is perfect; For all His ways are justice, A God of truth and without injustice; Righteous and upright is He. NKJV

Feel free to ask a lot of people to pray for something important. Paul did, and he said it made a difference.

2 Corinthians 1:11 He will rescue us because you are helping by praying for us. As a result, many will give thanks to God because so many people's prayers for our safety have been answered. NLT

Lesson Twenty-Four: Mercy

Lesson Twenty-Four is the first of two lessons which will focus on kingdom qualities explicitly linked to prayer. Unit Seven is called Forgive Us As We Forgive. The very first step in connecting with God will always be some form of asking for mercy. Jesus had a positive response for everyone who asked for mercy. He had a different response for those who wouldn't ask for mercy. One of the most poignant examples is found in Luke 18 in which Jesus shares two parables on prayer. In the second example, Luke 18:9-14, one person (a Pharisee) doesn't see any need to ask for mercy. The Pharisee based his "lack of need" on his "good behavior." The tax collector wouldn't even look up in his plea for mercy. We all know which one gained a hearing with God. We all need to let that concept soak into our souls. In order to be in a position to pray, and especially to teach others about prayer, we will need to get this right in our own soul first.

For the **HOOK ACTIVITY** in this lesson we will give the learners the opportunity to both ask for mercy and extend mercy. Use cards to illustrate giving "mercy." Each person that turns up a "diamond" is removed from the exercise, unless a person who turns up a heart allows them back into the exercise. The person who was removed has to ask for mercy. The person with a heart card extends, or doesn't extend, "mercy." Keep flipping cards, subsequently removing and reinstating players. Give the **impression** that the goal is to have the best Texas Holdem hand within the time limit. Set the time limit for this activity. When time runs out, the **actual winner** will be the person who extended mercy the most times. In case of **a tie** for the number of times mercy was extended, the person with the best Texas Holdem cards is the winner. If there are any concerns about using normal playing cards or playing Texas Holdem, use sets of Rook cards or Uno cards, and adjust the rules accordingly.

Transition to the **BOOK ACTIVITY** by saying that Jesus never turned away from someone who asked Him for mercy. We can see that expressed in every chapter of the book of Luke. Use the Have Mercy crossword activity from the student personal study guide. Almost all of the crossword answers are easily deduced from the Luke passages in the Across and Down columns, but like any crossword puzzle there will be some answers that are difficult. This activity can be done individually, in pairs, or in teams. Close this activity by highlighting that our approach to God begins with an understanding of our need for mercy. Jesus was clearly willing to extend mercy to those who asked for it. If we are going to become like Jesus, we need to have a similar default position in extending mercy to other people.

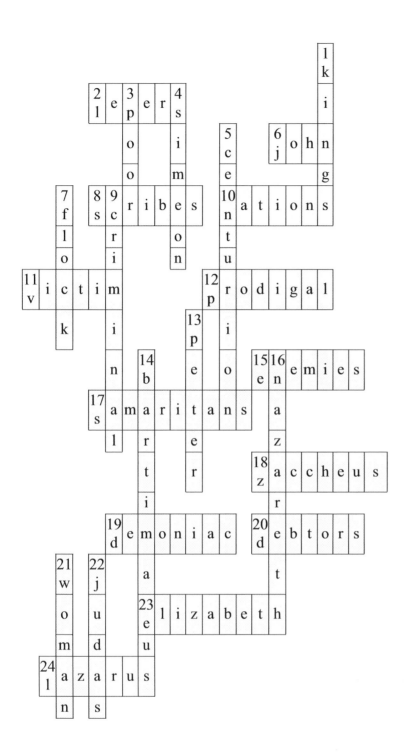

ACROSS

2. Luke 17:11-15

6. Luke 3:2-6

8. Luke 20:1-8

10. Luke 24:44-49

11. Luke 10:33-37

12. Luke 15-20-24

15. Luke 6:35-36

17. Luke 9:52-56

18. Luke 19:1-10

19. Luke 8:36-39

20. Luke 11:1-4,13

23. Luke 1:11-14,18,57-58

24. Luke 16:19-25

DOWN

1. Luke 21:12-15

3. Luke 14:21-24

4. Luke 2:25-31

5. Luke 7:2-10

7. Luke 12:27-32

9. Luke 23:39-43

13. Luke 5:8

14. Luke 18:38-43; Mark 10:46-52

16. Luke 4:16-21

21. Luke 13:10-13,16

22. Luke 22:48-51

Use the New King James Version for this exercise

ALTERNATE ACTIVITY: If the students have reviewed the student manual before class, you may want to use the Book of Luke Mercy Grab Bag Slips file. You can cut the page into slips that include the reference and lines for each chapter of the book of Luke. Have students pull slips from a grab bag and write down how mercy was demonstrated in that passage. They can then share their answers with the class.

The **LOOK ACTIVITY** for this lesson involves looking at how mercy was shown to Rachel in the Searching for Paradise 2 short story homework assignment. This should provide opportunity for the learners to project how we can see moments for extending mercy in people's lives. After they have identified how some of these characters extended or received mercy, you can challenge them to look for ways to extend mercy in their everyday lives. Here are some examples of how Rachel was shown mercy.

Mercy was shown to Rachel when Curtis went searching for her in Hawaii. She was shown mercy by Kalena, who helped her get a job, took her into her apartment, and invited her to Bubba Gump's. She was shown mercy by Gino, who gave her a place to stay after worship at the University of the Nations. She was also shown mercy by the custodian who allowed her to stay the night at the church. She was also shown mercy when she passed out on the beach. Some people took her into the cave and called the ambulance. She was also shown mercy when the nurse helped her with some clothes.

Once the class has shared their answers from the short story homework, you can invite them to make it more personal by sharing their own examples of having received mercy. How have they extended mercy to others? In order to get this discussion going you could share how God has shown mercy to you. You may want to use the following leading questions. Question one: How has God demonstrated mercy in your life? Question two: How have you demonstrated mercy in someone else's life?

For the **TOOK ACTIVITY** we will invite the class to share prayer requests for people who might need mercy…i.e., people for whom God might want you to intervene. Have them write the requests on 3 x 5 cards. There are many possible answers to this assignment. If they need to be prompted, you could ask if they know anyone who is sick or in need of a job. **Tell them that they shouldn't use any names**. They can **carefully record the need** or situation without using names. You could suggest that some people might need "mercy" for an upcoming test. Once the 3 x 5 cards are completed you could have them swap the cards with others in the class, and have them say: Will you pray for this person's need?

Memory Verse: Psalm 57:1,2 Have mercy on me, O God, have mercy on me, for in you my soul takes refuge. I will take refuge in the shadow of your wings until the disaster has passed. I cry out to God Most High, to God, who fulfills [his purpose] for me NIV

SESSION PLANNING SHEET

Session Title: _____Mercy_____ Date: _____

Session Focus: _God wants us to be merciful even as He is merciful. It is a character quality that God wants in our lives. __

Session Aims: **KNOW** _Recognize that our access to God begins with a posture of asking for and giving others mercy. __

           FEEL _ Express what it feels like to have or not have mercy extended to you. _____

           DO _ Make a commitment to pray each day for someone who needs God's mercy. _____

Session Plan	Session Activities	Preparation
Time:__15min__ APPROACH	**Methods, Instructions, Questions** **The heart of it all exercise** Use cards to illustrate giving mercy. Each person that turns up a "diamond" is removed from the exercise, unless a person who already turned up a "heart" allows them back in the exercise. The person who was removed has to ask for mercy. The person with a heart extends or doesn't extend "mercy." If you use Rook or Uno cards, choose colors to represent diamonds and hearts in this exercise.	**Materials** Deck of playing cards Or Rook cards Or Uno cards
Time:__20 min__ BIBLE EXPLORATION	**Book of Luke Mercy walk through exercise** Use Hebrews 4:16 to highlight our need to seek mercy and grace as we come to God in prayer. Highlight that Jesus was consistent in his response to people asking for mercy. Point to Luke 18:13 and how one person's prayer was accepted while the other person's prayer was not accepted. The difference was the heart attitude that called out for mercy, verses a heart attitude that didn't acknowledge any need for repentance. That's true in each of our lives as well. Suggest that there is a consistent response that Jesus had to the person asking for mercy. If we want to be like Jesus, we need a similar posture regarding extending mercy to people.	Bibles Student manuals Pens or pencils
Time:__15 min___ LIFE IMPLICATIONS	**It Is Finished Mercy Review** How was mercy demonstrated by God to the characters in the Searching For Paradise 2 short story? How did the characters in the story demonstrate mercy to others? (TEACHER) Consider Illustrating how God demonstrated mercy in your life by sharing your personal testimony. (STUDENTS) How has God demonstrated mercy in your life? How have you demonstrated mercy to others in your daily life?	Heaven Help Us short story from homework. Searching for Paradise 2
Time:__10 min__ APPLICATION	**Mercy Prayer requests (3 X 5 cards) <u>Without using names</u>**, or giving any indications of who the person might be, share a prayer request of someone who might be in need of God's mercy. God's mercy could involve any kind of need. Ask how many would like God's help with an upcoming test? Exchange cards and have volunteers pray for the need expressed on the card. For some groups, the leader might need to pray for the requests. Highlight that a person's need of salvation is where mercy begins. **OR Take open personal prayer requests and have students pray for each other.**	3x5 index cards

Unit Seven –Forgive Us Our Debts – Lesson 24 – Mercy…Prompts10

The best thing you can do with personal insult, injury, or injustice, is to present it to God, protect yourself from further harm and go peacefully on your way. The best thing you can do for others facing insult, injury or injustice is to pray them, and then help as God directs.

Matthew 5:44 But I say, love your enemies! Pray for those who persecute you! NLT

Micah 6:8 No, O people, the LORD has already told you what is good, and this is what he requires: to do what is right, to love mercy, and to walk humbly with your God. NLT

Revival will come as the people of God humble themselves and pray for it. God has committed that responsibility to His people. If our hearts are broken about the state of our country, we must stand up, speak up and kneel.

2 Corinthians 5:19,20 namely, that God was in Christ reconciling the world to Himself, not counting their trespasses against them, and He has committed to us the word of reconciliation. Therefore, we are ambassadors for Christ, as though God were making an appeal through us; we beg you on behalf of Christ, be reconciled to God NASB

Boldness can be described as being fearless, courageous, daring, and confident. Answered prayer is not found in the place of doubt and fear. When is the last time you heard or offered a truly bold prayer?

Hebrews 4:16 Let us therefore come boldly unto the throne of grace, that we may obtain mercy, and find grace to help in time of need. NKJV

The day may come when we feel as if God has turned His back on us. He hasn't. God's answers may not come early, but they are never late. We need to fill our minds with that truth.

Lamentations 3:8,21,22 Even when I call out or cry for help, he shuts out my prayer. Yet this I call to mind and therefore I have hope: Because of the LORD's great love we are not consumed, for his compassions never fail. NIV

There is a prayer that will be ignored by God, and one that won't. It's not hard to figure out. Now go and do accordingly.

Luke 18:11,13 The proud Pharisee stood by himself and prayed this prayer: 'I thank you, God, that I am not a sinner like everyone else, especially like that tax collector over there! For I never cheat, I don't sin, I don't commit adultery. "But the tax collector stood at a distance and dared not even lift his eyes to heaven as he prayed. Instead, he beat his chest in sorrow, saying, 'O God, be merciful to me, for I am a sinner.' NLT

Have you ever been trapped outside in a violent lightning storm, in waves that threaten to sink your boat, or in a "white out" snow storm? In a situation like that we cry out for mercy and look for any kind of shelter that might be available. Our sin has placed us in such a position before the Holy God. The cross has provided the shelter we so desperately need.

Psalm 57:1,2 Have mercy on me, O God, have mercy on me, for in you my soul takes refuge. I will take refuge in the shadow of your wings until the disaster has passed. I cry out to God Most High, to God, who fulfills [his purpose] for me NIV

There should be a somber side of prayer. We need to recognize that lives hang in the balance. That is the case in any warfare. If the cause is just, there are people who need to be rescued and set free. It would all be just too deadly serious, "But God." But God who is rich in mercy…But God who loves us…But God who has rescued us…But God Who has won the victory…But God!

Ephesians 2:4,5 But God, being rich in mercy, because of His great love with which He loved us, even when we were dead in our transgressions, made us alive together with Christ (by grace you have been saved) NASB

Lesson Twenty-Five: Forgiveness

Lesson Twenty-Five is the second of two lessons which will focus on kingdom qualities emphatically linked to prayer. Unit Seven is called Forgive Us As We Forgive. In today's lesson we will look at how indispensable forgiveness is to our prayer life. As we learned in the last lesson, the very first step in connecting with God will always be some form of asking for mercy. Today we will find that asking for mercy is the first step in a process that leads to a full and vibrant relationship with God. As the instructor for this lesson, I highly recommend that we spend some time in personal reflection before teaching this lesson. Every person on the planet has probably had a "forgiveness issue" to deal with. That is the nature of the world in which we presently exist. Fortunately, as Christians we hope for a "better world."…one in which righteousness dwells. But, for now, we live in this world and there will be "tribulation." Learning to walk through the pain, the wonder, and glory of forgiveness is a lesson worth learning. We must understand the foundation of this truth from the very beginning. Jesus was clear that our being forgiven is directly related to our extending forgiveness. Matthew 6:12,14-15 $_{NIV}$ puts it this way: ***And forgive us our debts, as we also have forgiven our debtors.*** *For if you forgive other people when they sin against you, your heavenly Father will also forgive you.* ***But if you do not forgive others their sins, your Father will not forgive your sins.*** Mark 11:25 $_{NIV}$ states it this way: *And when you stand praying,* ***if you hold anything against anyone, forgive them, so that your Father in heaven may forgive you your sins.*** Matthew 18:35 $_{NIV}$ says it this way: ***This is how my heavenly Father will treat each of you unless you forgive your brother or sister from your heart.*** Ephesians 4:32 $_{NIV}$ frames this truth in this way: *Be kind and compassionate to one another,* ***forgiving each other, just as in Christ God forgave you.*** Colossians 3:13 $_{NIV}$ echoes what was said to the Ephesians: *Bear with each other and forgive one another if any of you has a grievance against someone.* ***Forgive as the Lord forgave you.*** There is no ambiguity in Scripture on this matter. So, from the start, let's accept that fact that not forgiving others is not an option. That is a pretty hard truth to wrap our heads and hearts around. It can be even more difficult to "live that out" on a daily basis. Let's explore that along with our students.

For the **HOOK ACTIVITY** in this lesson we will help the students learn the consequences for holding on to bitterness and being unwilling to forgive. We will illustrate this truth through the clenched fist exercise. You will want to test out the length of time that you have the students "clench the fist." This exercise can be a little dangerous if you press the clinched fist for too long. Have one of the students clench their fist as hard as they can. You can distract them by saying that part of the exercise includes having another student slowly and gently rub the inside of their wrists. After an appropriate amount of time, ask them to unclench their fist. If you do this for the correct amount of time, the student will have a hard time actually opening their fist. The fingers temporarily lock in the clenched position. This is a great illustration of how bitterness or "lack of forgiveness" will place our emotions in a locked position. If held too long, we will find it more and more difficult to open our hearts from the clenched position.

Transition to the **BOOK ACTIVITY** by suggesting that Jesus helped us gain a deeper understanding of forgiveness by illustrating it through parables found in Matthew 18 and Luke 7. We can also gain some insight on this topic from King David and what he shared in Psalm 51. We will use the Forgiveness Step Ladder exercise to help us understand how we can get to a place of true freedom. The students should have already worked on this with the Student Personal Study Guide, but if they don't have study guides you can use the Forgiveness Step Ladder worksheet from the teacher's resource CD. In this exercise there is a lighter area to the left of the steps where they can enter the portions that best represent that element of the Steps to Freedom. The following represents the elements from each of the passages.

Psalm 51:10-13　　　**Psalm 51:18-19**　　**Psalm 51:1-4**　　　**Psalm 51:5-9**　　　**Psalm 51:14-17**

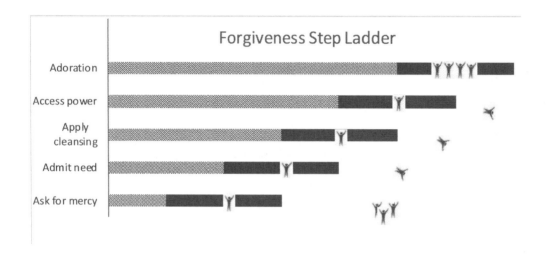

Psalm 51:18-19	Step 5	Adoration	
Psalms 51:14-17	Step 4	Access power for change	It could include 1,2.
Psalm 51-10-13	Step 3	Apply cleansing	It could lead to steps 4 & 5.
Psalm 51:5-9	Step 2	Admit need	It could reflect steps 1, 3, 4.
Psalm 51:1-4	Step 1	Ask for mercy	It could include step 2.

Mathew 18:31-33   Matthew 18:34-35   Matthew 18:21-26   Matthew 18:27-30

Person was unable to attain Step 5

Matthew 18:34-35   **Failure on Step 3…must return to Step 1.**

Matthew 18:27-30   **They skipped Step 2 and failed on Step 3…must return to Step 1.**

Matthew 18:31-33   **Failure on Step 2...must return to Step 1.**

Matthew 18:21-26   **Steps 1 & 2**

Move on to the **LOOK ACTIVITY** by continuing to use the Forgiveness Step Ladder exercise. Utilize the parable from Luke 7 as an illustration of our need to assess where we are in the area of forgiveness. Have the students identify where they think the guests (Pharisees) were on the Forgiveness Step Ladder. Have the students assess where they think Simon was on the step ladder. Where do they think the woman was on the Forgiveness Step Ladder? In a moment of quiet reflection, have the students tell God where they are on that ladder.

Luke 7:36-38   Luke 7:44-46   Luke 7:47-48   Luke 7:39-43   Luke 7:49-50

Guests - Luke 7:49-50   Failure on Steps 1-5…they must begin at Step 1.

Simon - Luke 7:44-48   Failure on Steps 1-5…he must begin at Step 1.

Woman – Luke 7:47-48   Success on Step 3…she may be at Steps 4 & 5.

Simon - Luke 7:39-43   Failure on Steps 1-5…he must begin at Step 1.

Woman - Luke 7:36-38   Success on Steps 1 & 2.

For the next exercise match the scripture reference to the words of the verse.
This can be found in this week's Prayer Prompts homework assignment.

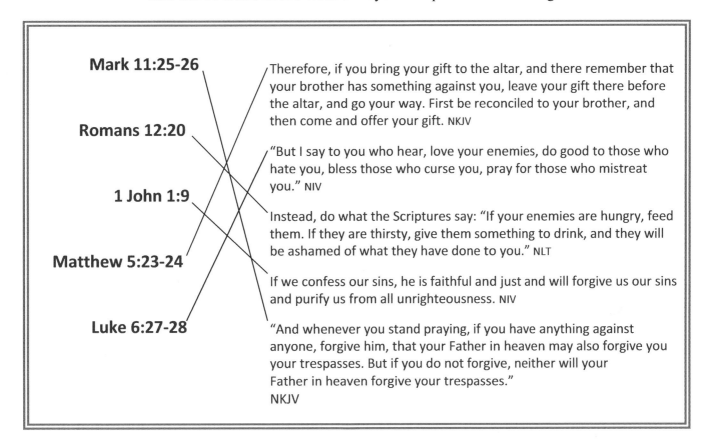

Mark 11:25-26

Therefore, if you bring your gift to the altar, and there remember that your brother has something against you, leave your gift there before the altar, and go your way. First be reconciled to your brother, and then come and offer your gift. NKJV

Romans 12:20

"But I say to you who hear, love your enemies, do good to those who hate you, bless those who curse you, pray for those who mistreat you." NIV

1 John 1:9

Instead, do what the Scriptures say: "If your enemies are hungry, feed them. If they are thirsty, give them something to drink, and they will be ashamed of what they have done to you." NLT

Matthew 5:23-24

If we confess our sins, he is faithful and just and will forgive us our sins and purify us from all unrighteousness. NIV

Luke 6:27-28

"And whenever you stand praying, if you have anything against anyone, forgive him, that your Father in heaven may also forgive you your trespasses. But if you do not forgive, neither will your Father in heaven forgive your trespasses." NKJV

For the **TOOK ACTIVITY** suggest that the students humbly ask God for help in moving to the next step of the ladder. Tell them that God (and you) would be available to help them with any questions they have about how to make it to the next step. Provide the students with a 3 x 5 prayer reminder cards that they could use each morning of the coming week. It should record what God would like them to do in their desire to move up the Forgiveness Step Ladder. God desires that we all enjoy a vibrant relationship with Him (Adoration level).

In some settings this would be a good place to share in **communion**.

Or in other settings, you might close this session with a song of PRAISE.

Memory Verse: Ephesians 4:32 And be kind to one another, tenderhearted, forgiving one another, even as God in Christ forgave you. NKJV

SESSION PLANNING SHEET

Session Title: _When You Stand Praying Forgive_____ Date: _____

Session Focus: _Identify the steps that must be taken to develop a vibrant relationship with God. _____

Session Aims: **KNOW** _ Identify Scriptures which teach us that forgiving others is an essential step in our access to God. _

   FEEL _ Express a willingness to ask for and also extend forgiveness to others. _____

   DO _ Reflect on what our next step towards a more vibrant relationship with God might involve. _____

Session Plan	Session Activities	Preparation
Time:__10 min__ APPROACH	**Methods, Instructions, Questions** **Clenched Fist Exercise** Have students clench their fist for 60 seconds while their partner rubs their wrist. When 60 seconds are up, ask them to open their hands. Our spirits can be like those clenched fists. If we close them off long enough, it will be very difficult to un-clench them.	**Materials**
Time:__25 min__ **BIBLE EXPLORATION**	**Forgiveness Step Ladder Exercise** PSALM 51 & Matthew 18:21-35 Step 1 Ask for mercy Step 2 Acknowledge your need Step 3 Application of a cleansing process Step 4 Creation of a new heart (transformation) Step 5 Thanksgiving & praise Step 6 Extend your hand to help others gain (forgiveness) What happens when a person doesn't get a broken bone properly set? What happens when a person doesn't get a wound properly cleansed?	Bibles, Pens or Pencils, Student Personal Study Guides Or Forgiveness Step Ladder Worksheet
Time:__15 min___ **LIFE IMPLICATIONS**	**Forgiveness Step Ladder Exercise personalized** Luke 7:36-50 Where were the Pharisees (guests) on the Forgiveness Step Ladder? Where was Simon on the Forgiveness Step Ladder? Where was the woman on the Forgiveness Step Ladder? Reflection Point Where do you believe you are at on the Forgiveness Step Ladder? In some settings you may choose to serve Communion.	Bibles, Pens or Pencils, Student Personal Study Guides Or Forgiveness Step Ladder Worksheet
Time:__10 min__ APPLICATION	Personal Prayer – Humbly ask God what will be needed to take you up to the next level on the Forgiveness Step Ladder. Write down God's response on a 3 x 5 Prayer reminder card to be reviewed each morning of the coming week. If appropriate for your setting close today's session with a song of praise and thanksgiving.	Music for closing song Audio amplification if needed

Session Planning Sheet ©2013 Dale Roy Erickson, adapted from material found in *Creative Bible Teaching* © 1998 by Lawrence O. Richards and Gary J. Bredfeldt, Moody Publishers. Used by permission.

Unit Seven –Forgive Us Our Debts – Lesson 25 – Forgiveness…Prompts

Most people get more than one opportunity to demonstrate love and blessing to their enemies. Today is a good day for that. A good place to start is to ask God to bless them in our times of prayer.

Luke 6:27,28   "But I say to you who hear, love your enemies, do good to those who hate you, bless those who curse you, pray for those who mistreat you.   NIV

Have you ever experienced the power that saying "I forgive you" or "Will you forgive me?" has in a relationship? We should go there more often.

Mark 11:25,26   "And whenever you stand praying, if you have anything against anyone, forgive him, that your Father in heaven may also forgive you your trespasses. But if you do not forgive, neither will your Father in heaven forgive your trespasses."   NKJV

The simple words "I'm sorry" can carry a great blessing. They will likely bless you, the person you say them to, your family, the family of God, and open the doors of heaven.

Matthew 5:23,24   Therefore if you bring your gift to the altar, and there remember that your brother has something against you, leave your gift there before the altar, and go your way. First be reconciled to your brother, and then come and offer your gift.   NKJV

We have all heard of spiritual leaders or parents or bosses who have done horrible things to others. You might even have experienced some form of this yourself. There is only one response that will bring healing to our souls. We forgive them and pray for them. What happens to them is in God's hands.

Psalm 35:12,13   They repay me with evil for the good I do. I am sick with despair. Yet when they were ill, I grieved for them. I even fasted and prayed for them, but my prayers returned unanswered.   NLT

There are some blessings from God that only get released when we pray for those who have wounded us.

Job 42:10   When Job prayed for his friends, the LORD restored his fortunes. In fact, the LORD gave him twice as much as before!   NLT
Romans 12:20   Instead, do what the Scriptures say: "If your enemies are hungry, feed them. If they are thirsty, give them something to drink, and they will be ashamed of what they have done to you."   NLT

Meaningful prayer is connected to my relationships with others…in demonstrating love, grace and forgiveness.   The best place to start is in the kitchen.

1 Peter 3:7   Husbands, in the same way be considerate as you live with your wives, and treat them with respect as the weaker partner and as heirs with you of the gracious gift of life, so that nothing will hinder your prayers.   NIV

Here is a great way to finish off the year. Take all the sins, failures, regrets, mistakes, hurtful words spoken and received and cast them into the sea of forgetfulness. Of course, the first and last step of getting that done is seeking forgiveness from God and those who were hurt in the process.

1 John 1:9   If we confess our sins, he is faithful and just and will forgive us our sins and purify us from all unrighteousness.   NIV
Micah 7:19   You will again have compassion on us; you will tread our sins underfoot and hurl all our iniquities into the depths of the sea.   NIV

Made in the USA
Lexington, KY
20 November 2019